HERE WE ARE

PANOS KOKKINIAS

With text by Régis Durand,
Susan Kismaric,
and Alexandra Moschovi

powerHouse Books • BROOKLYN, NY

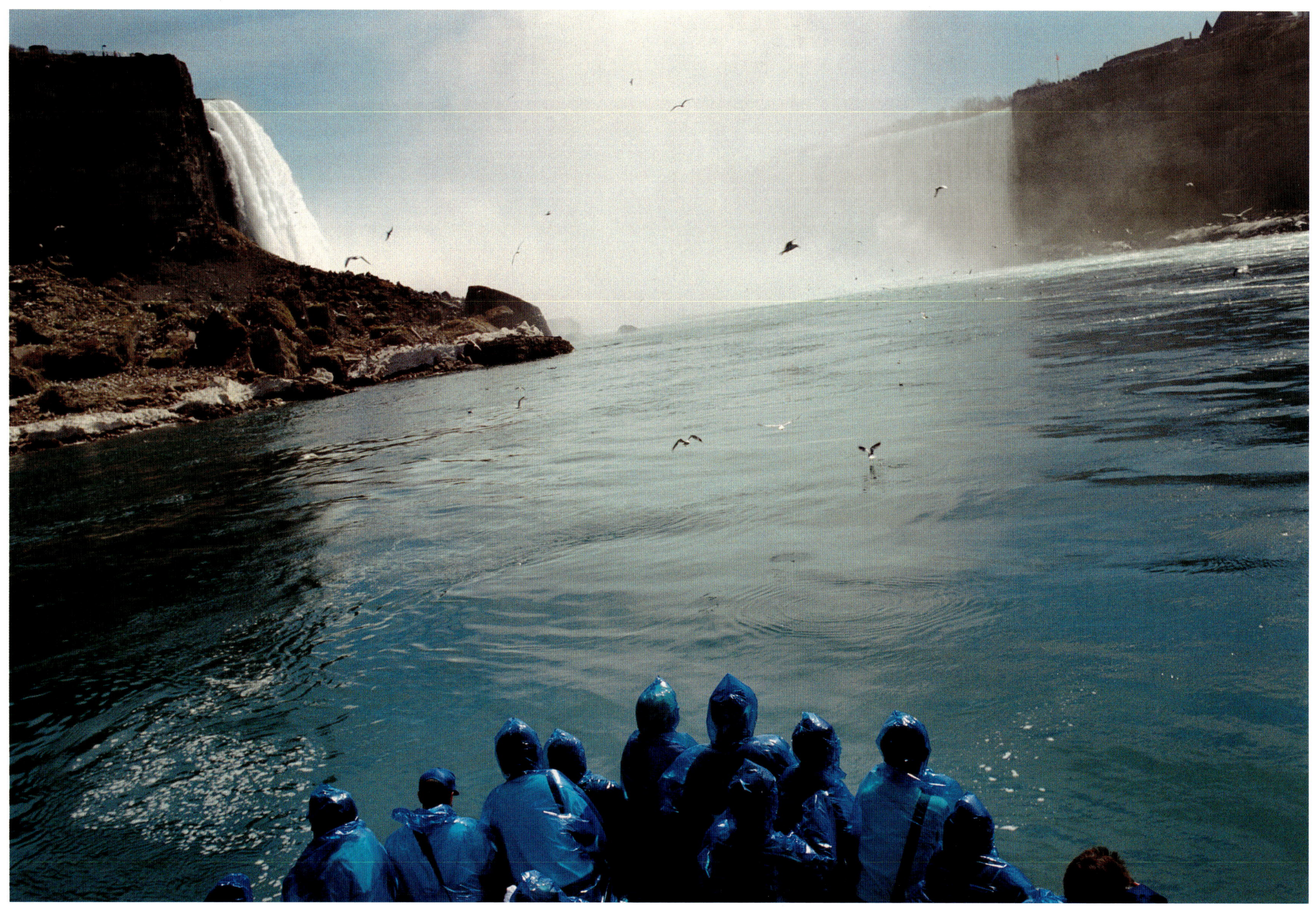

CONTENTS

HOME

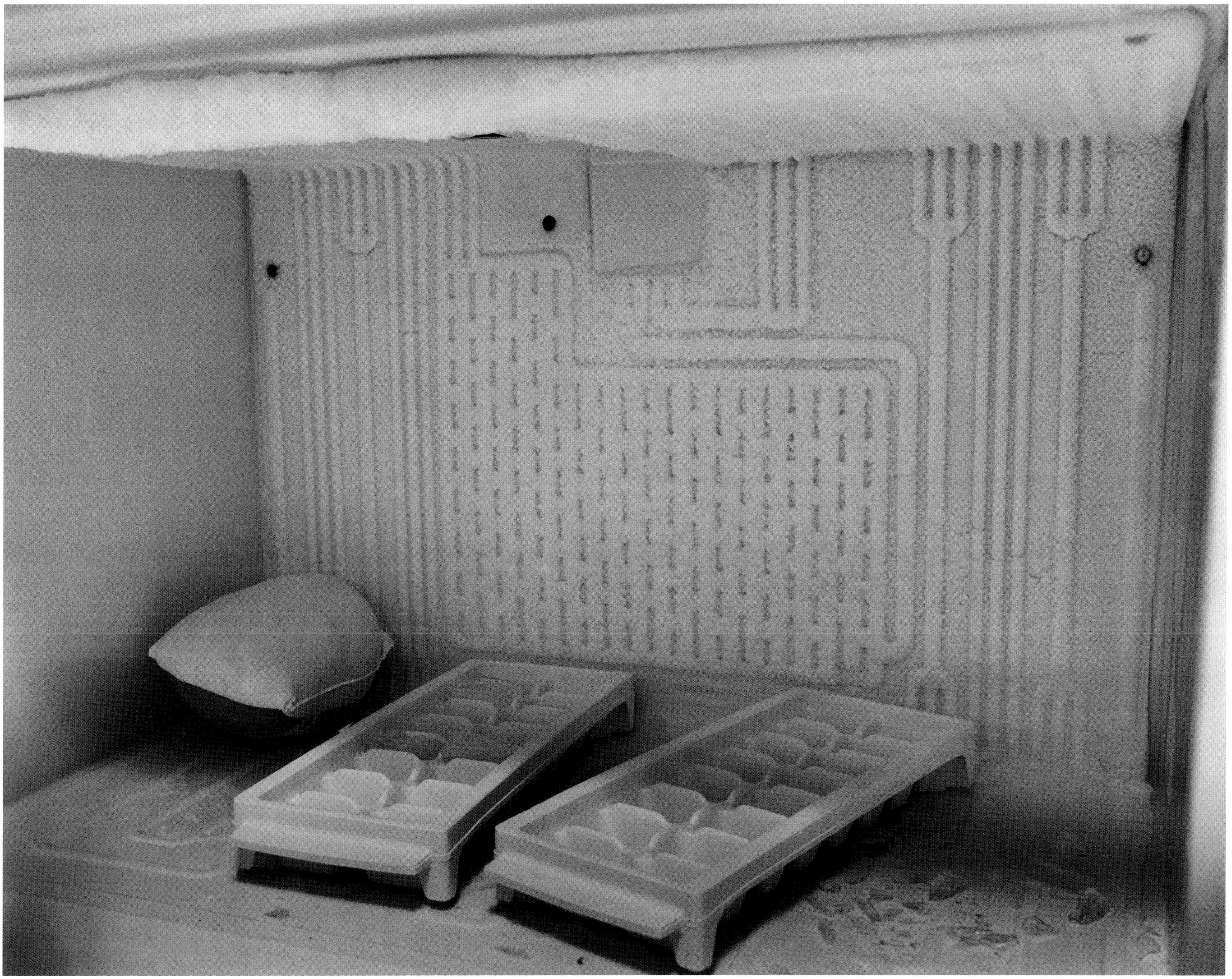

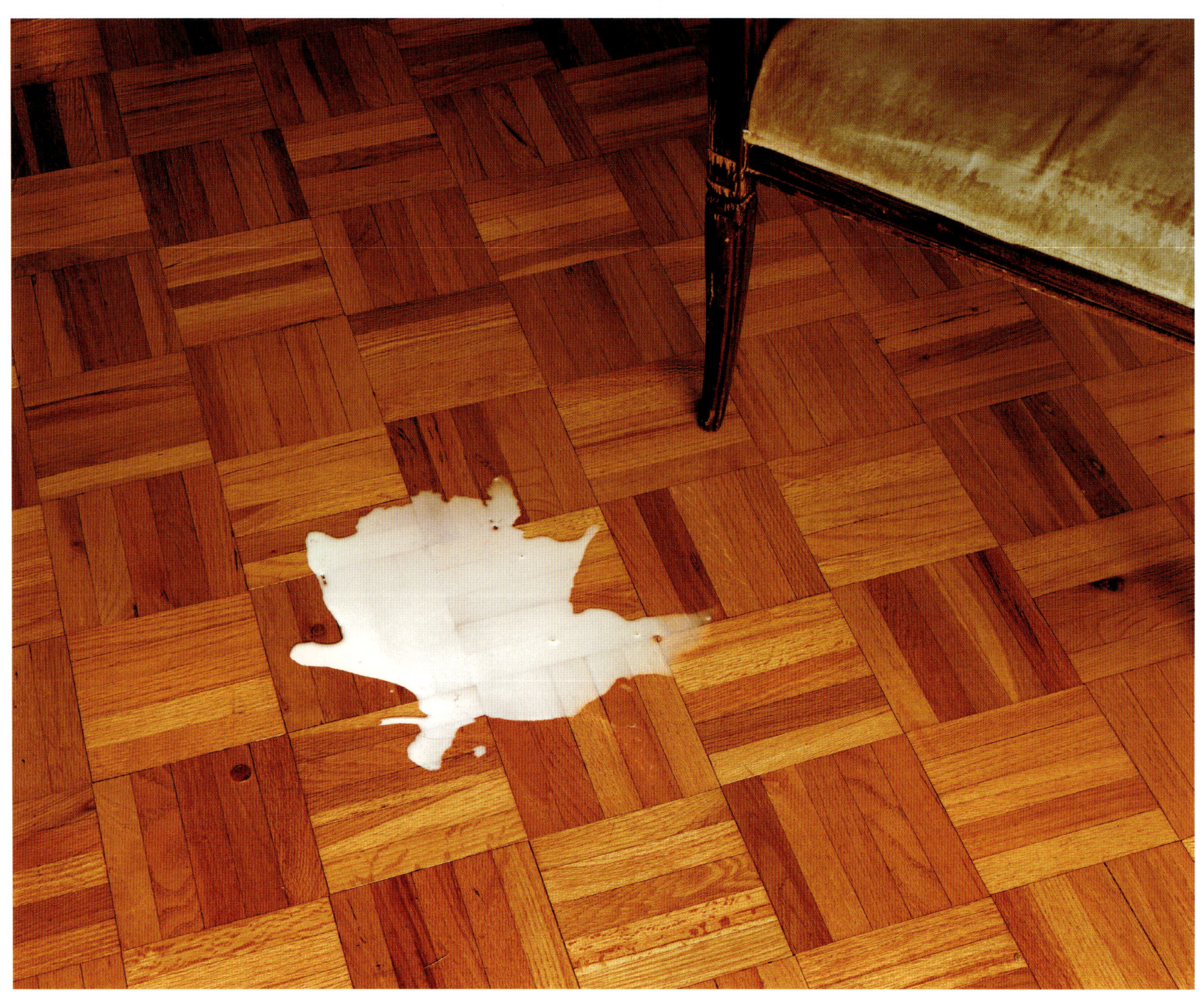

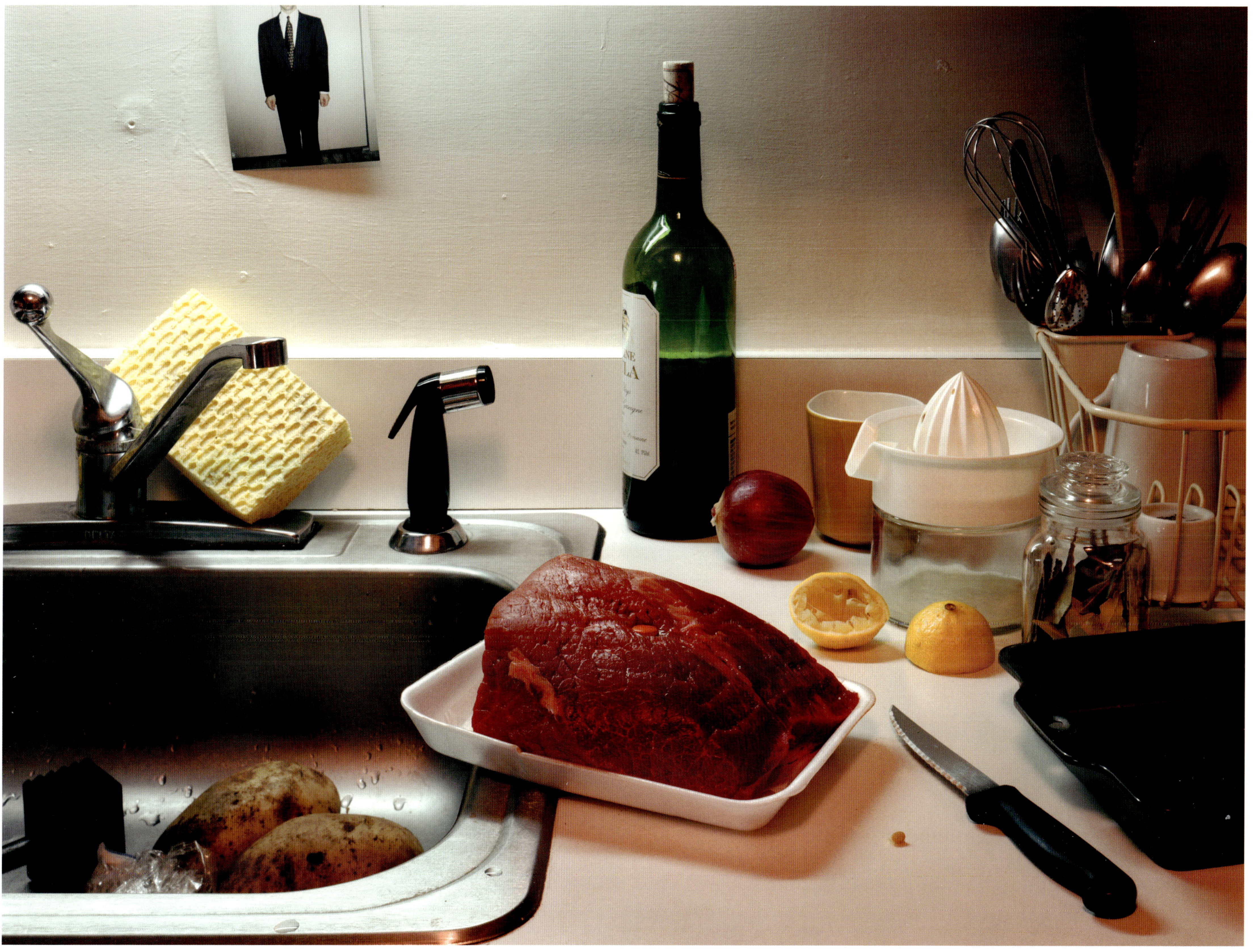

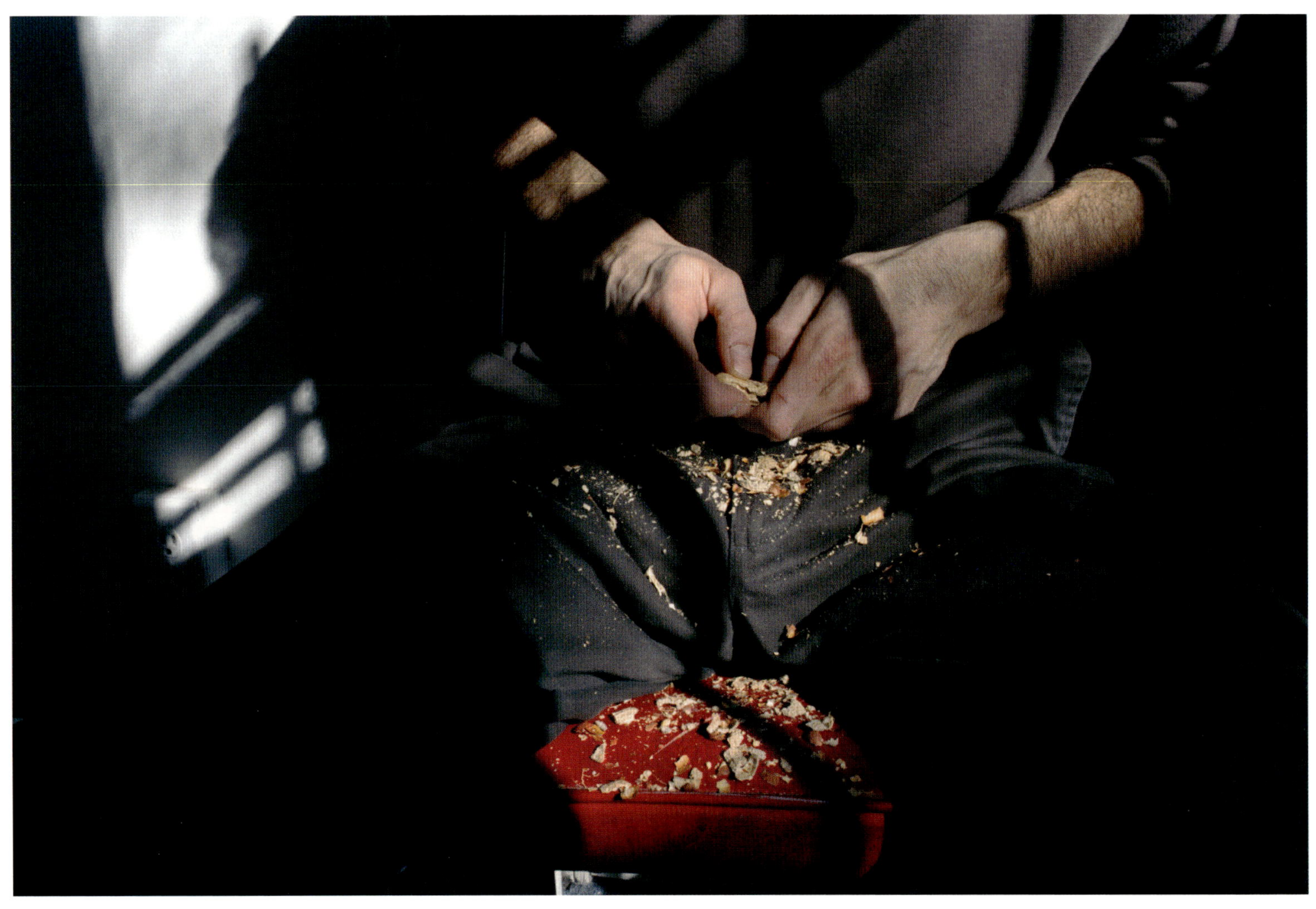

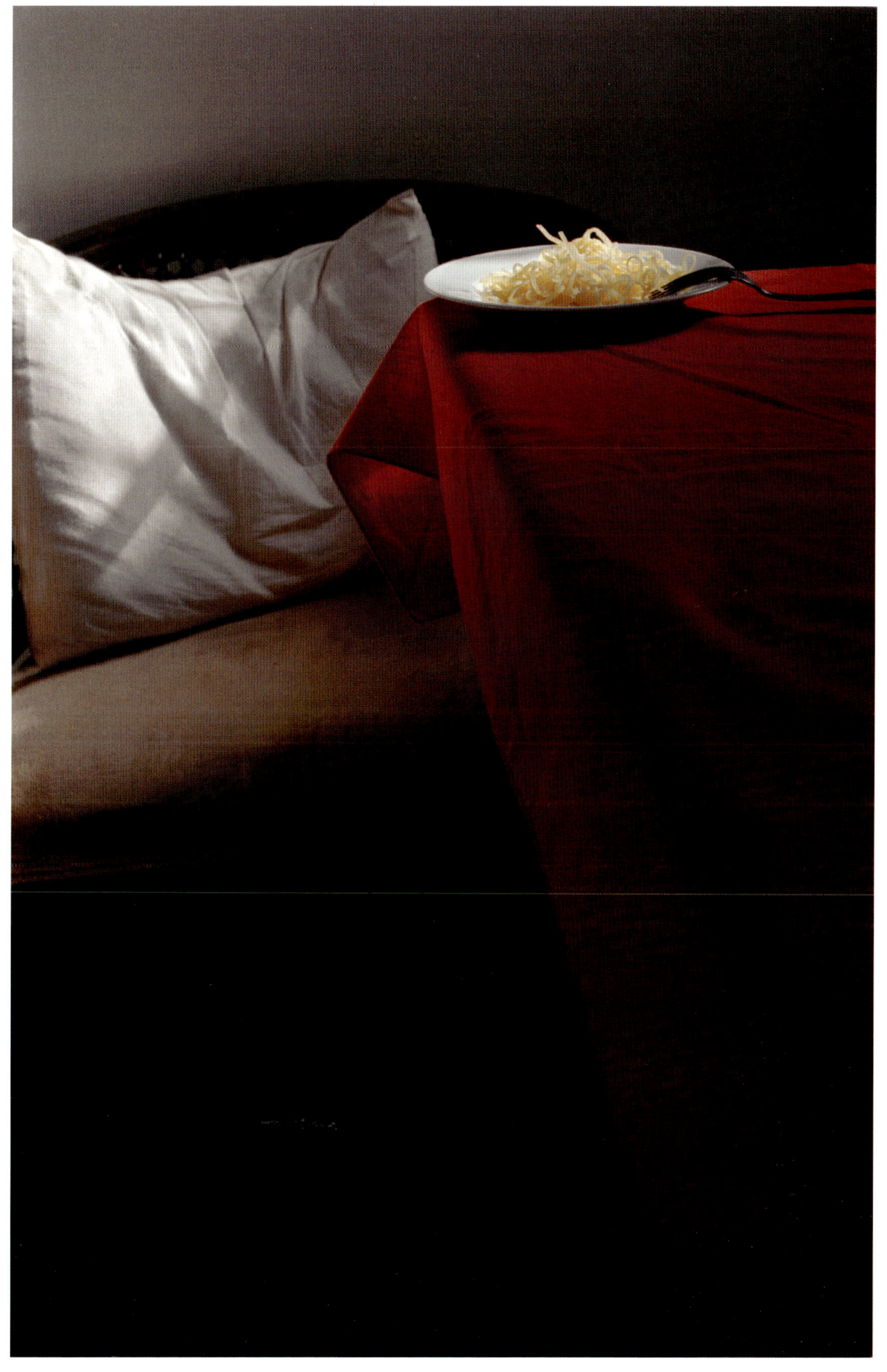

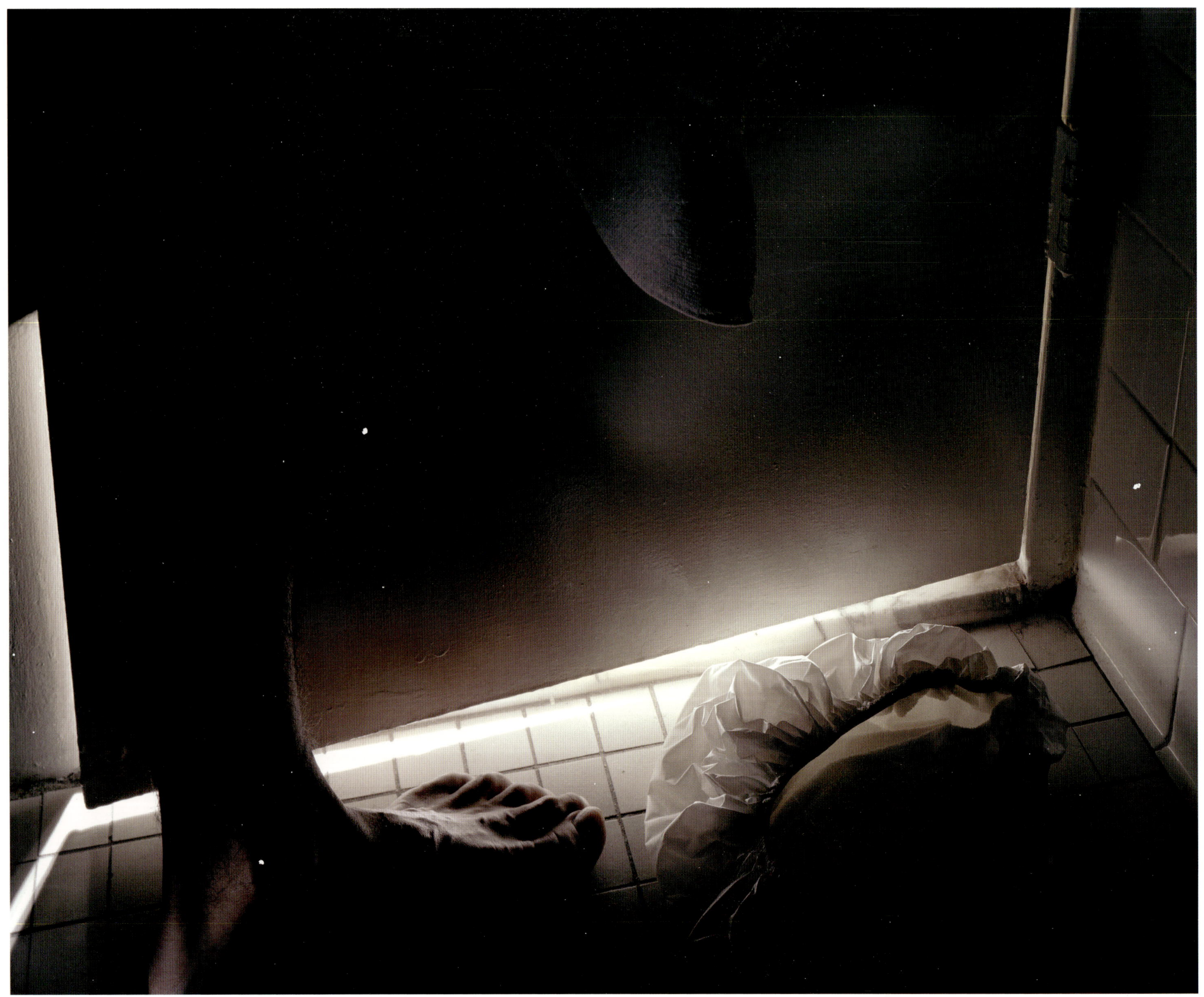

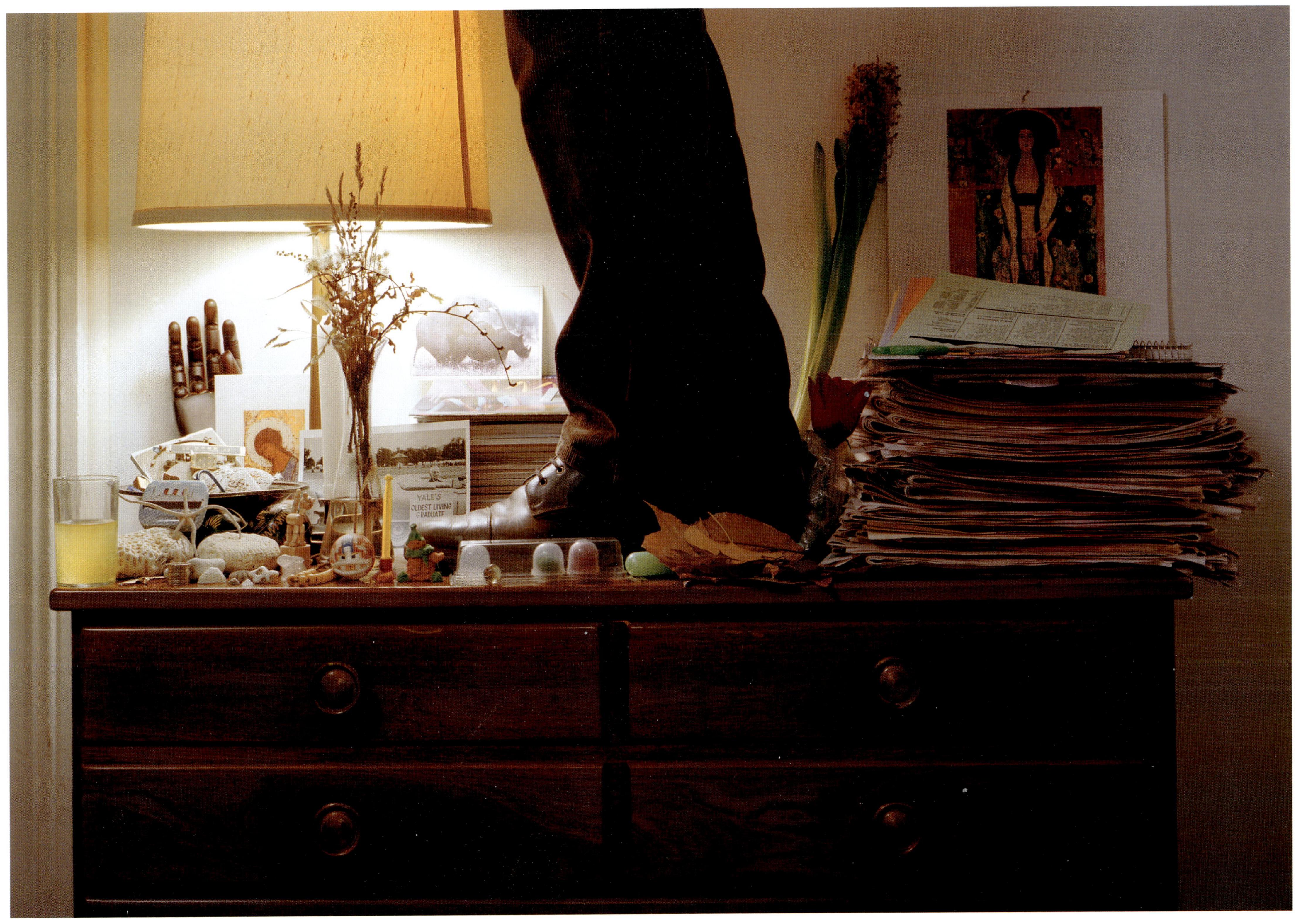

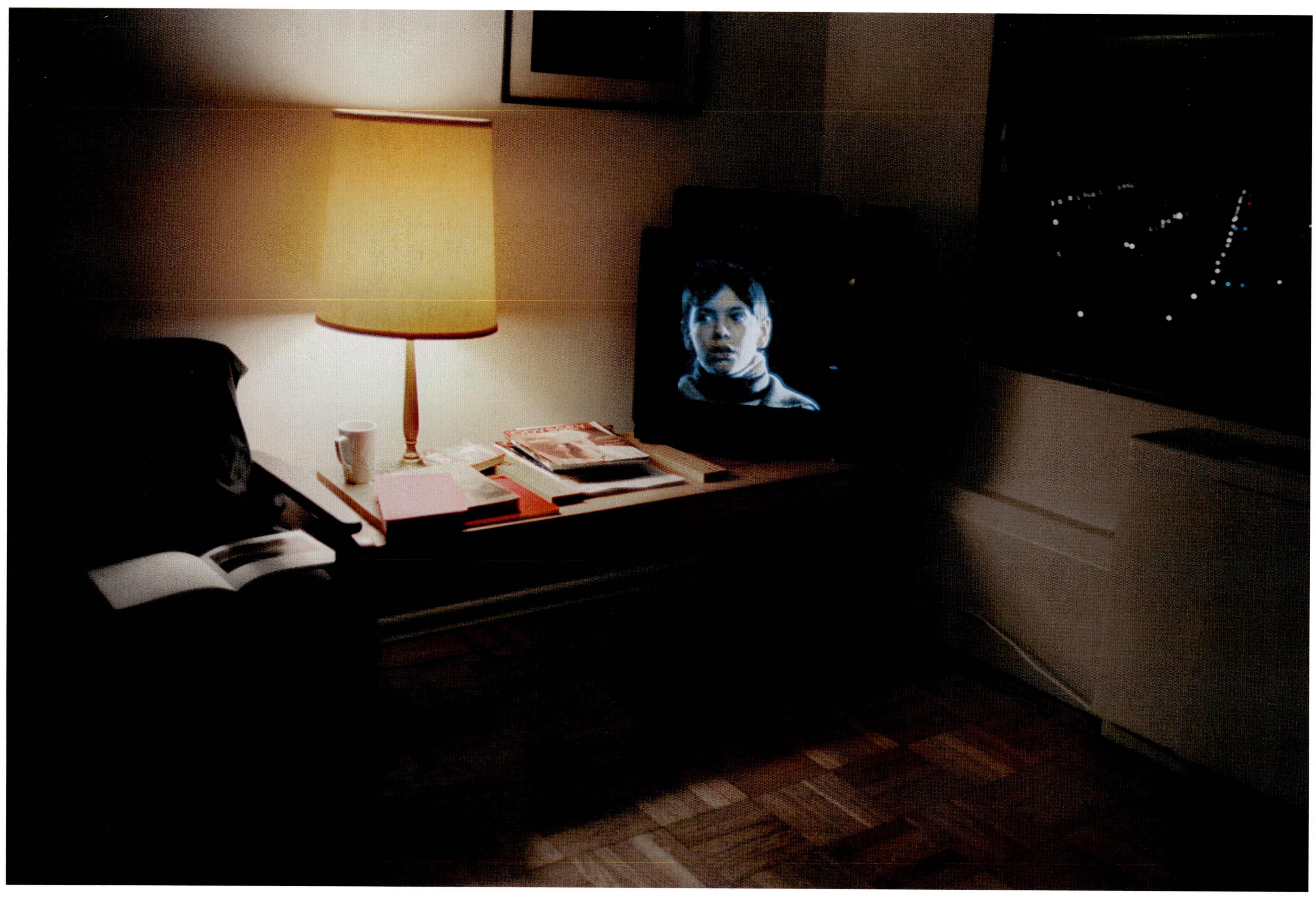

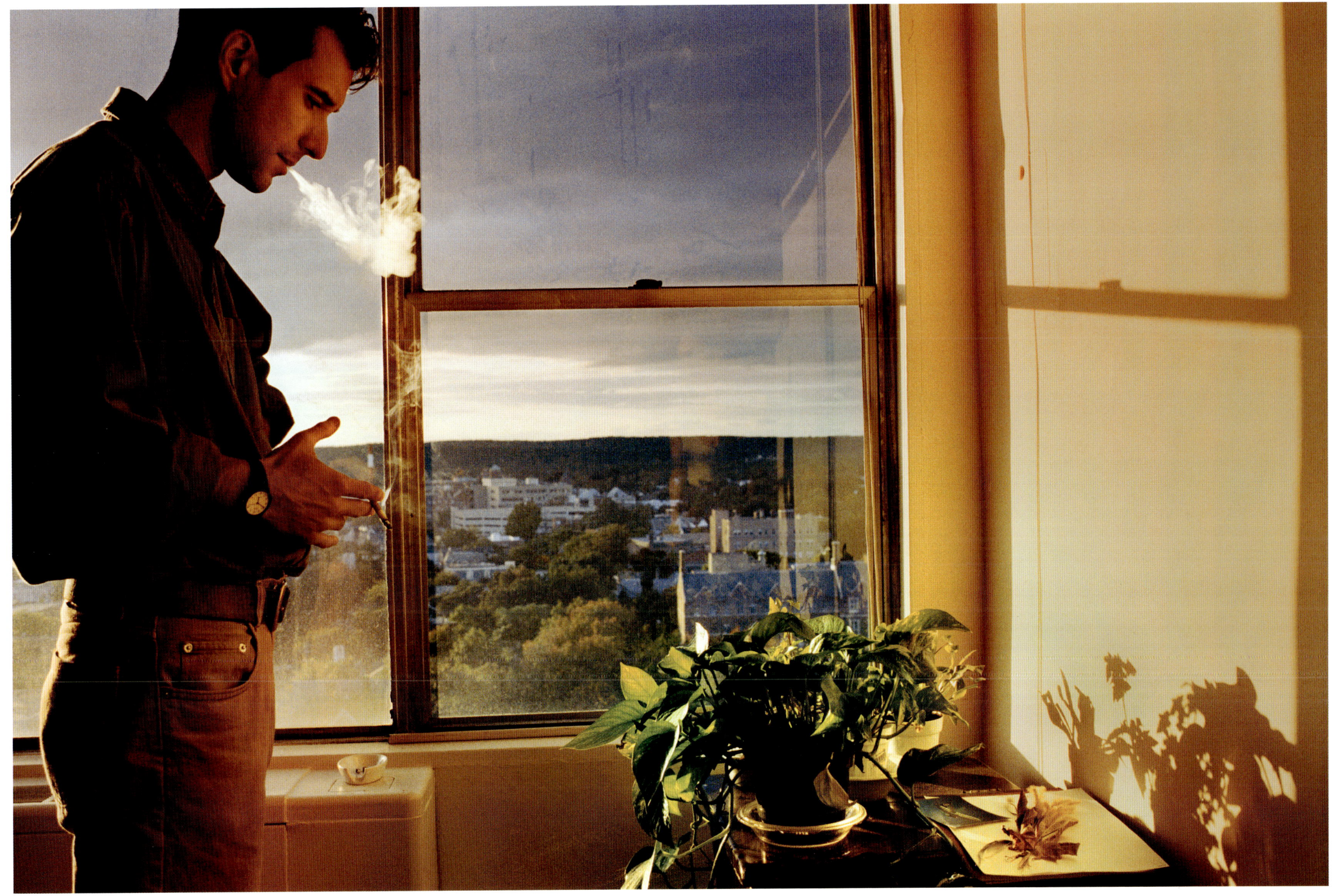

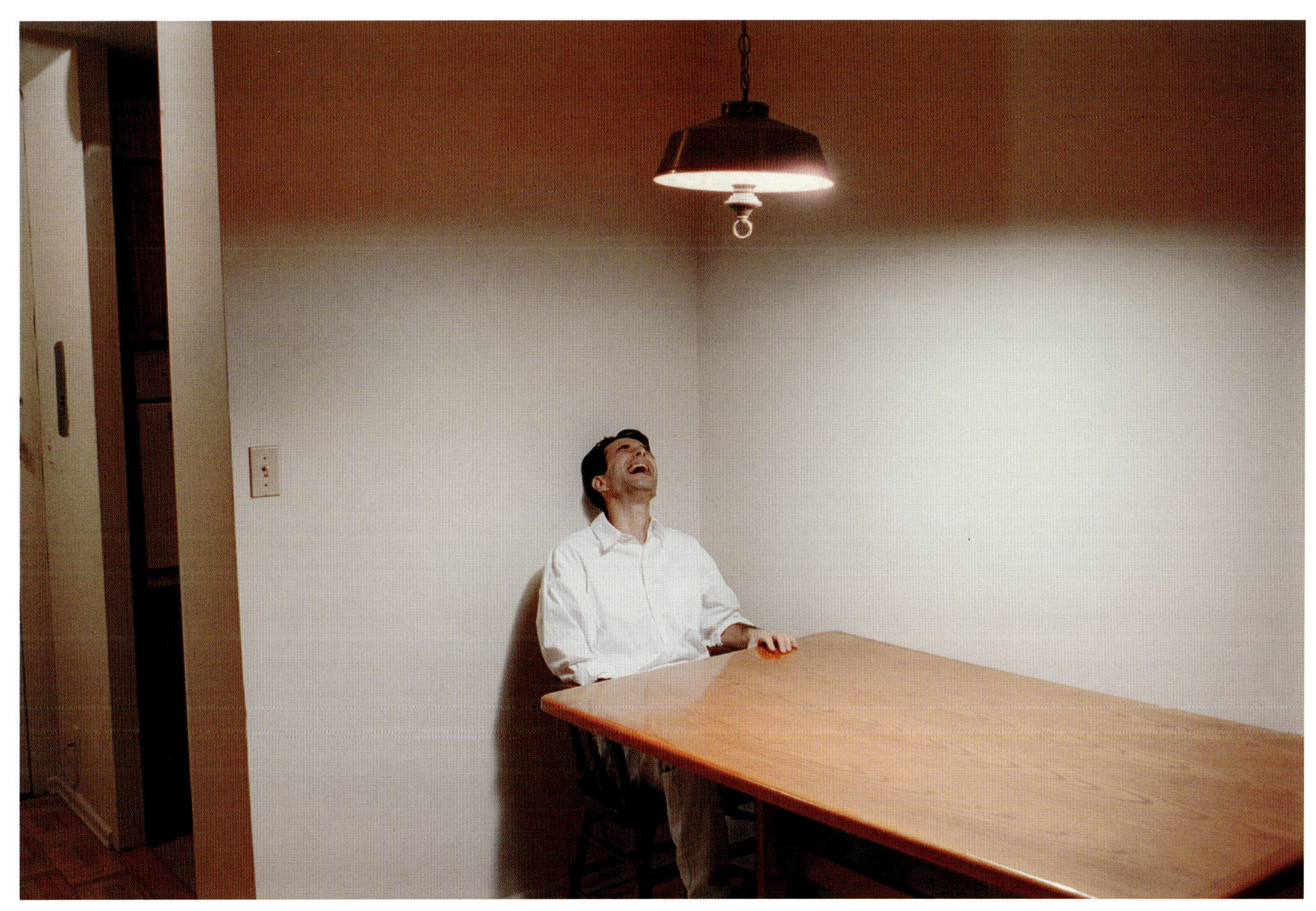

INTERIORS

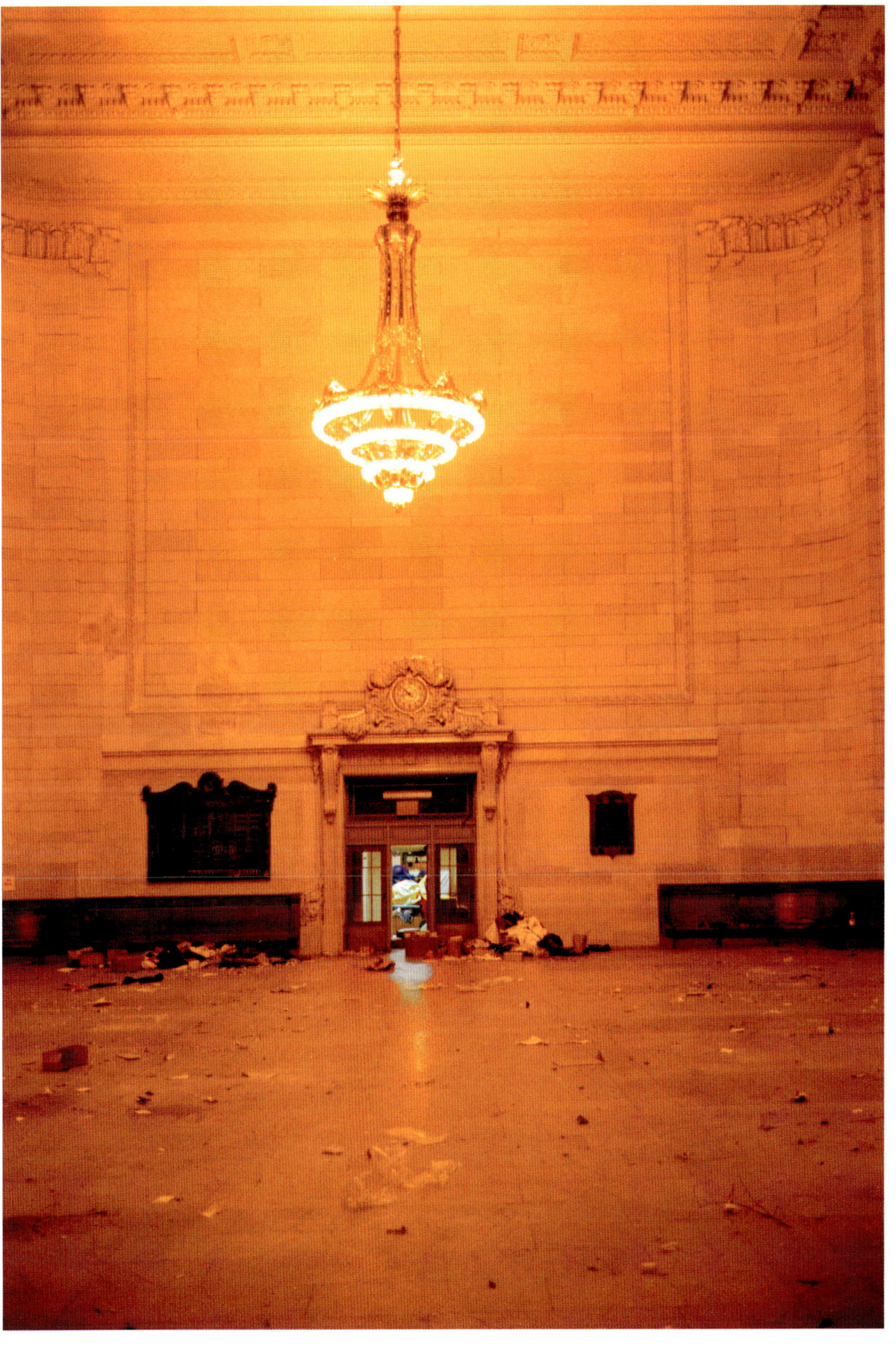

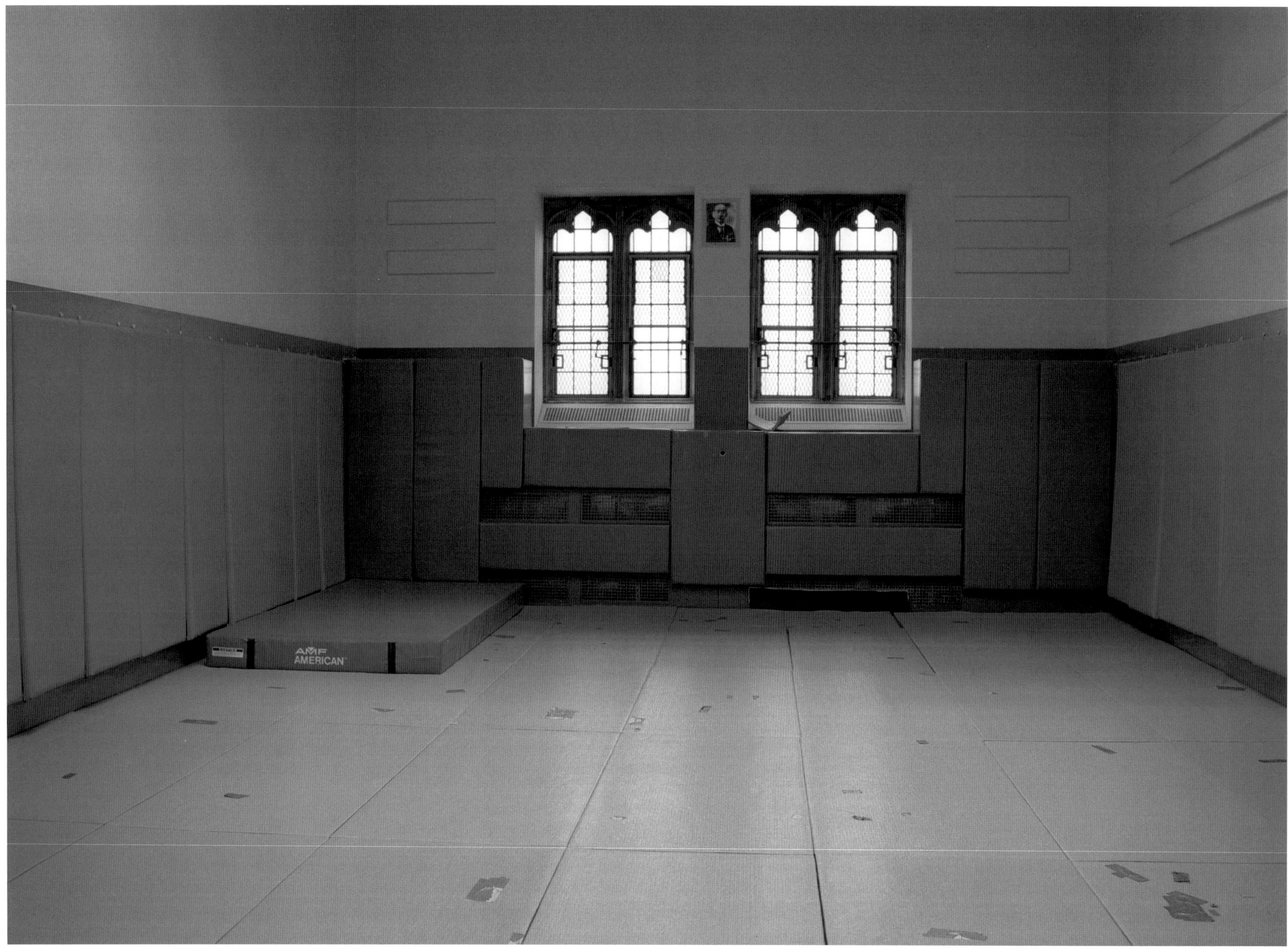

22 / Blue Room

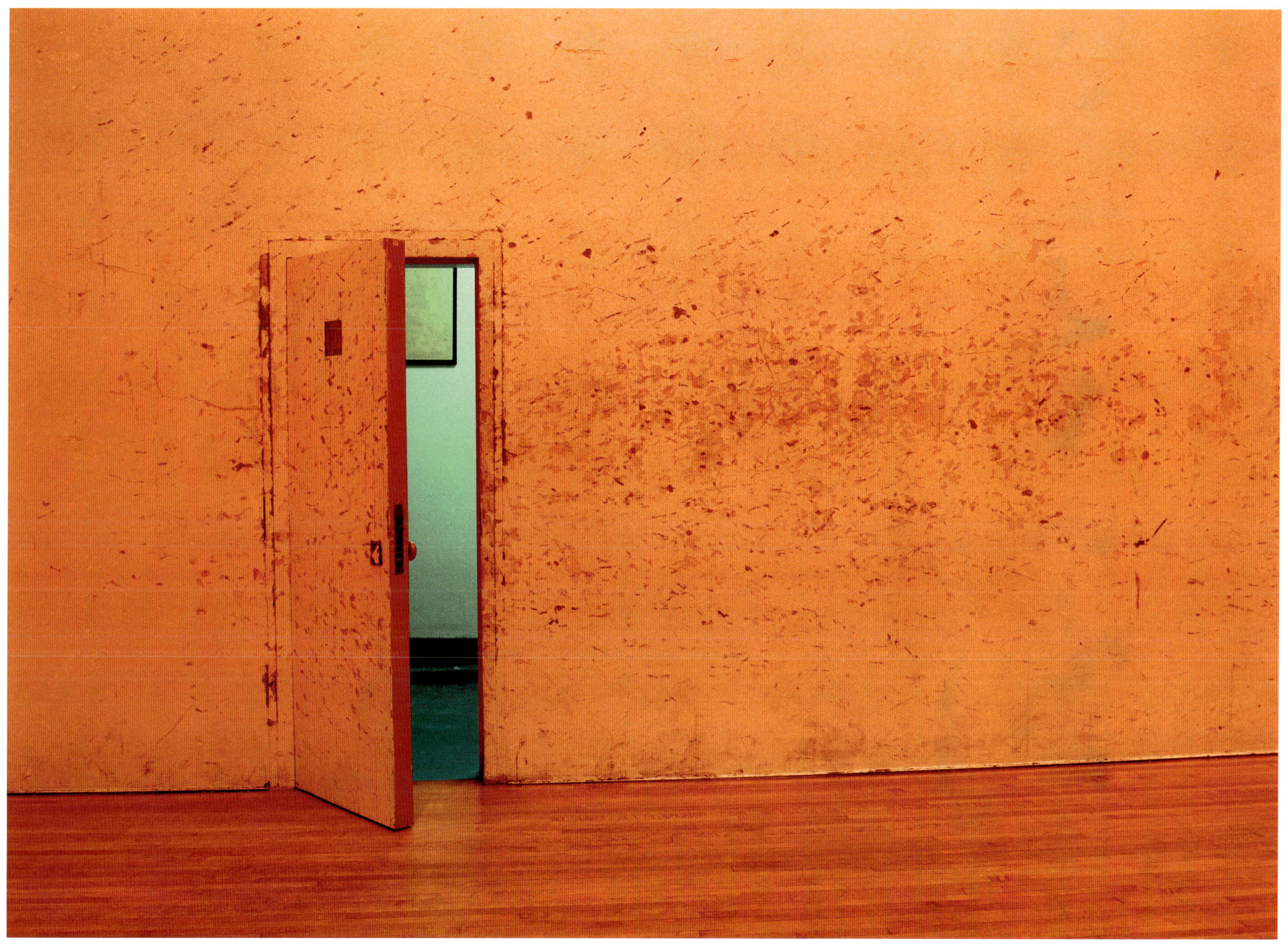

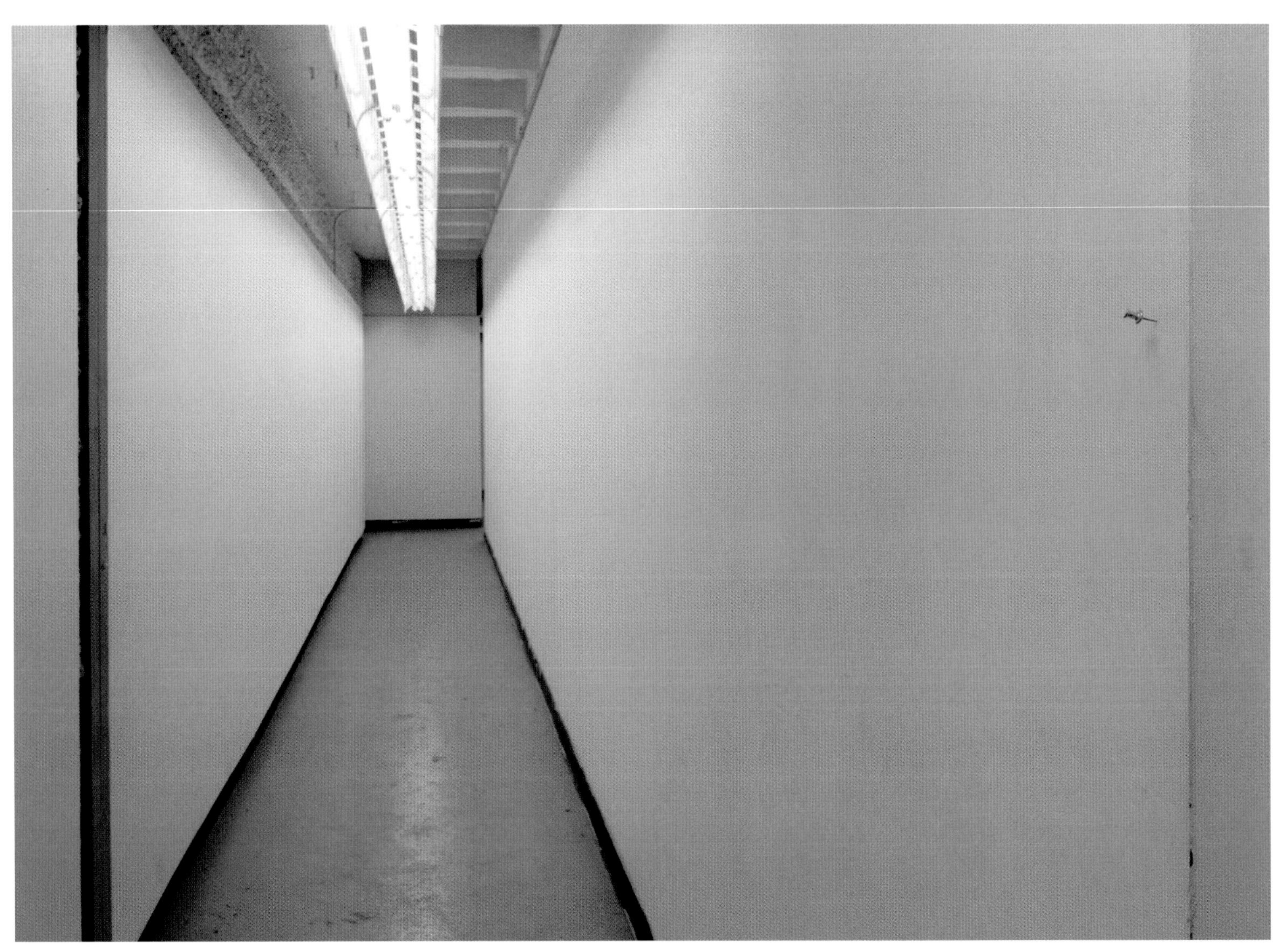

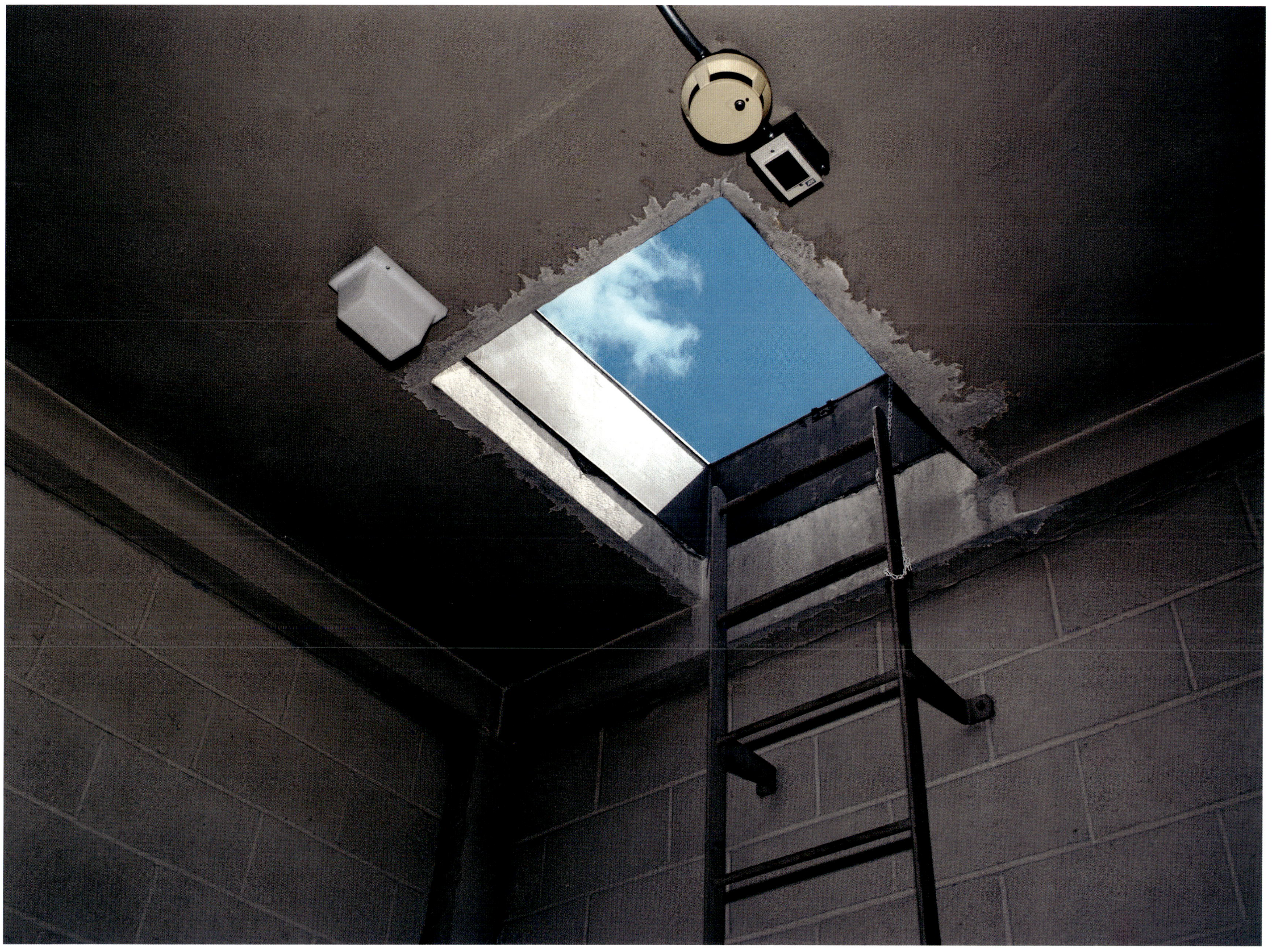

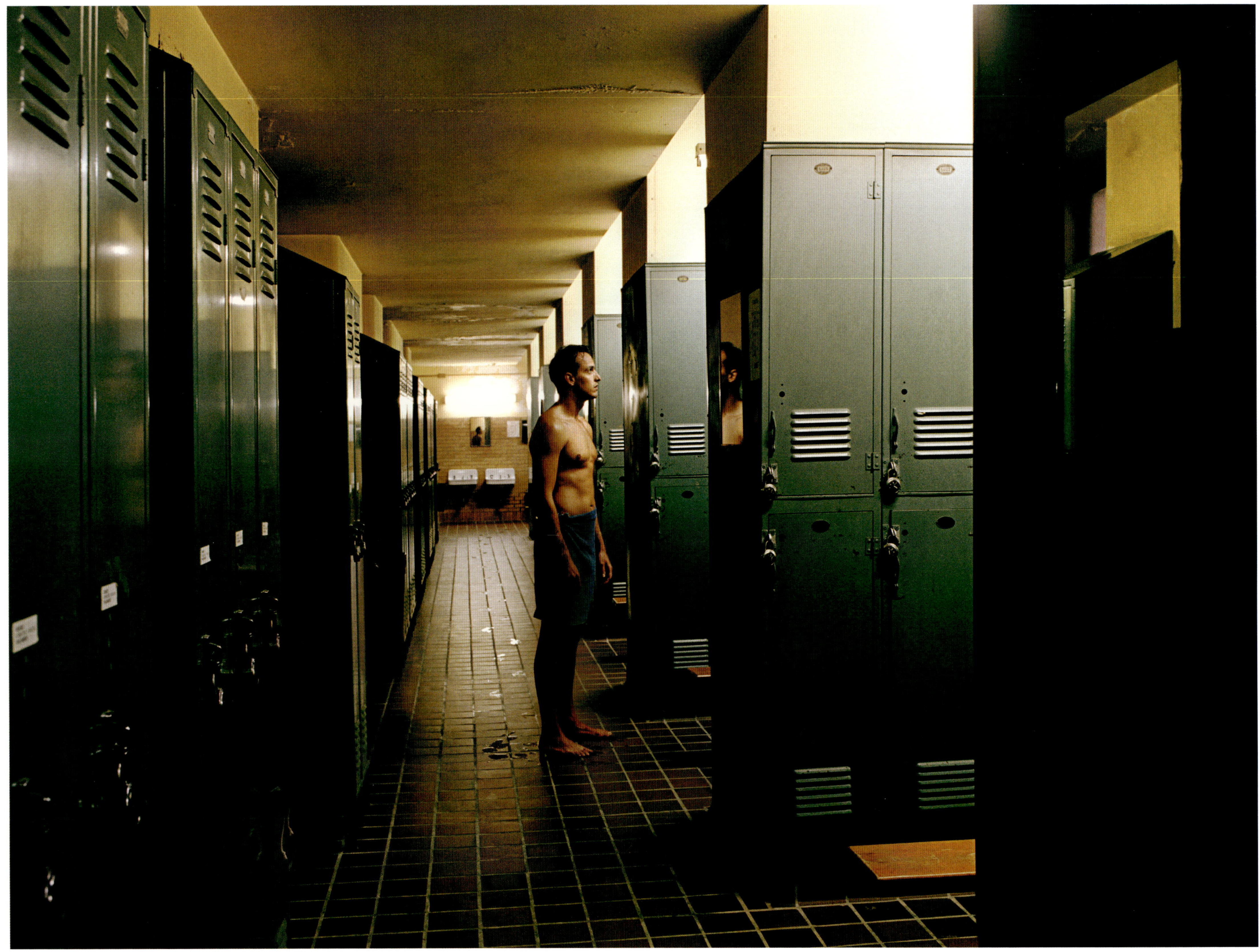

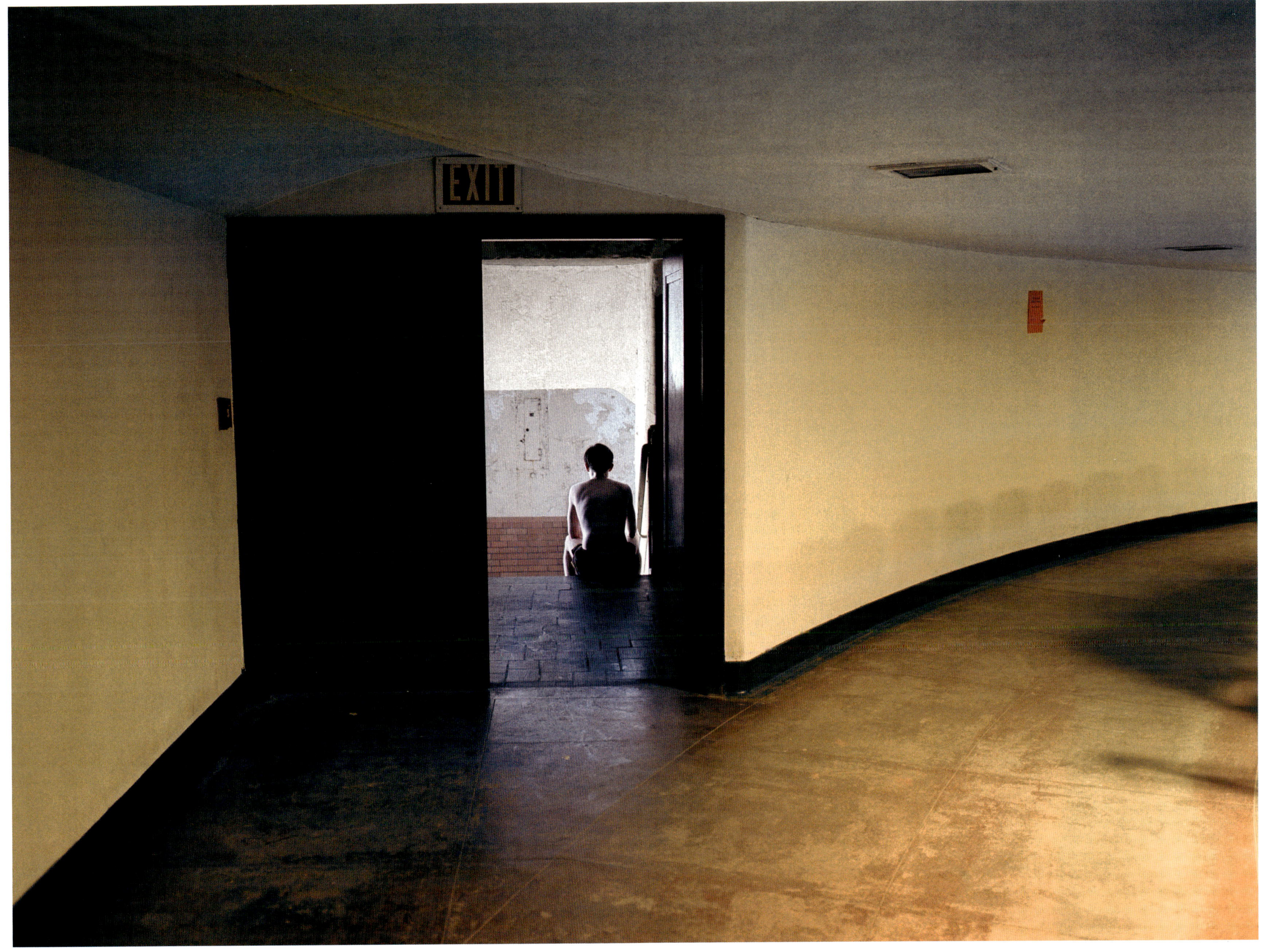

EXIT

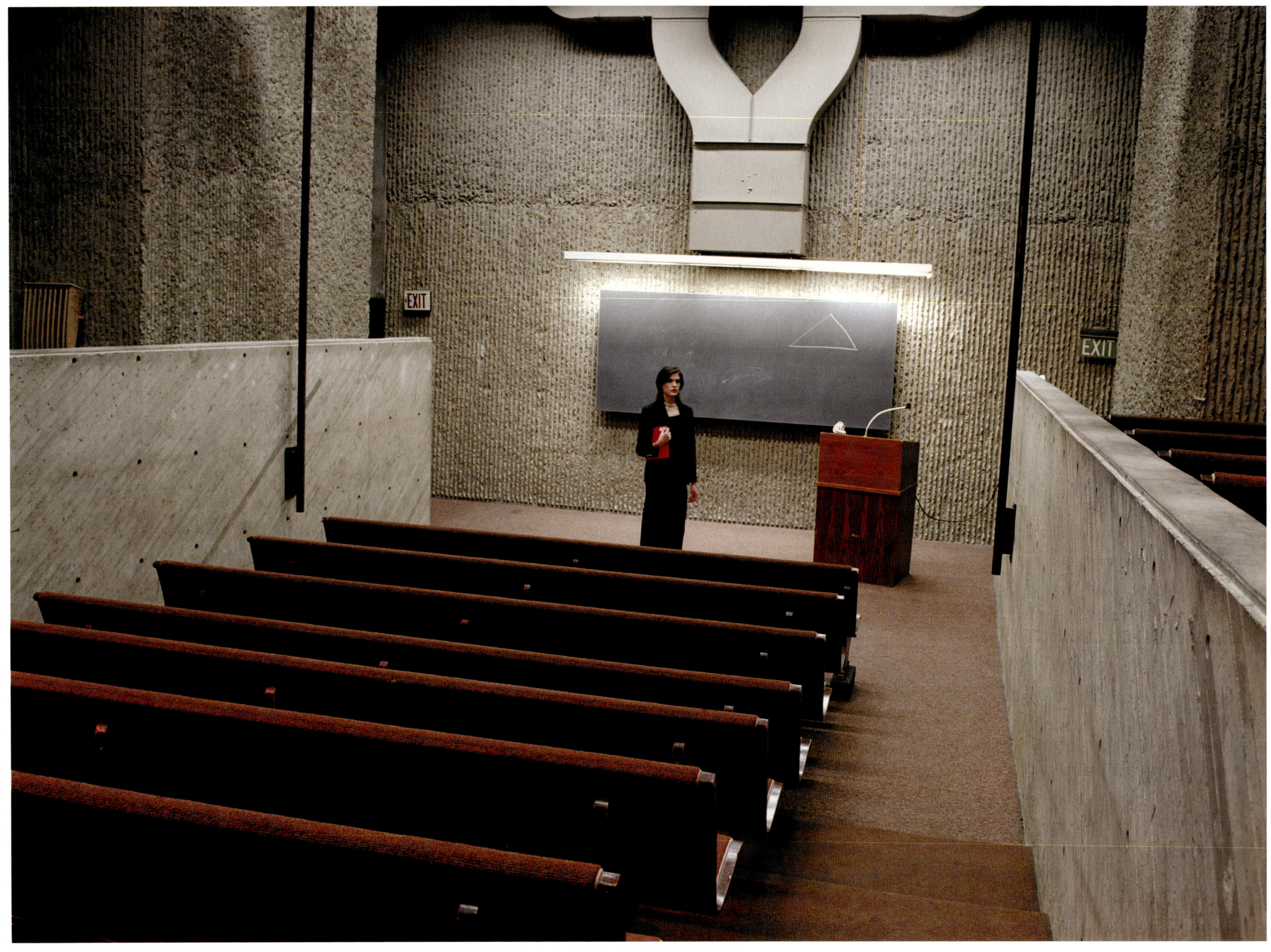

28 / Dana

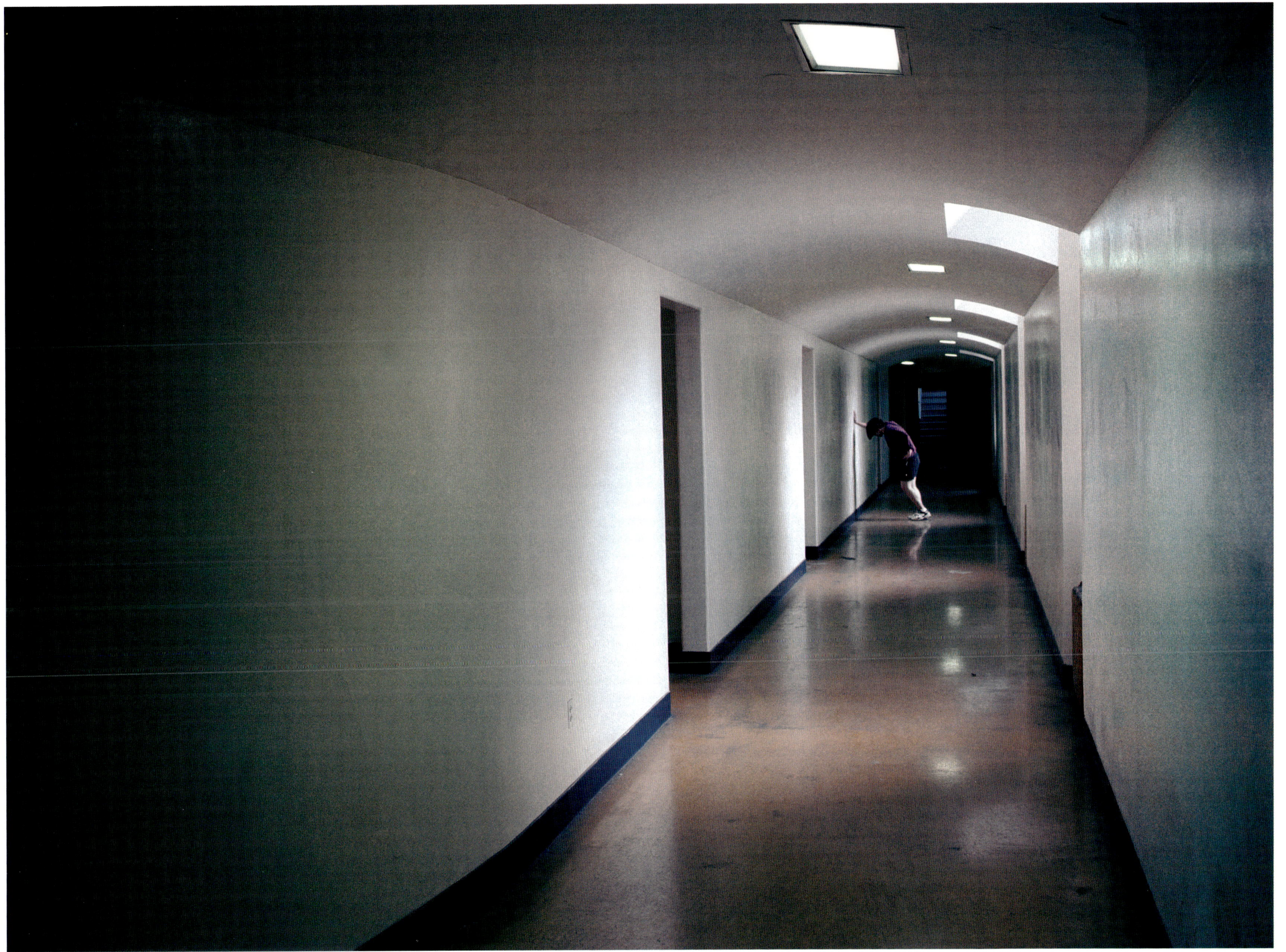

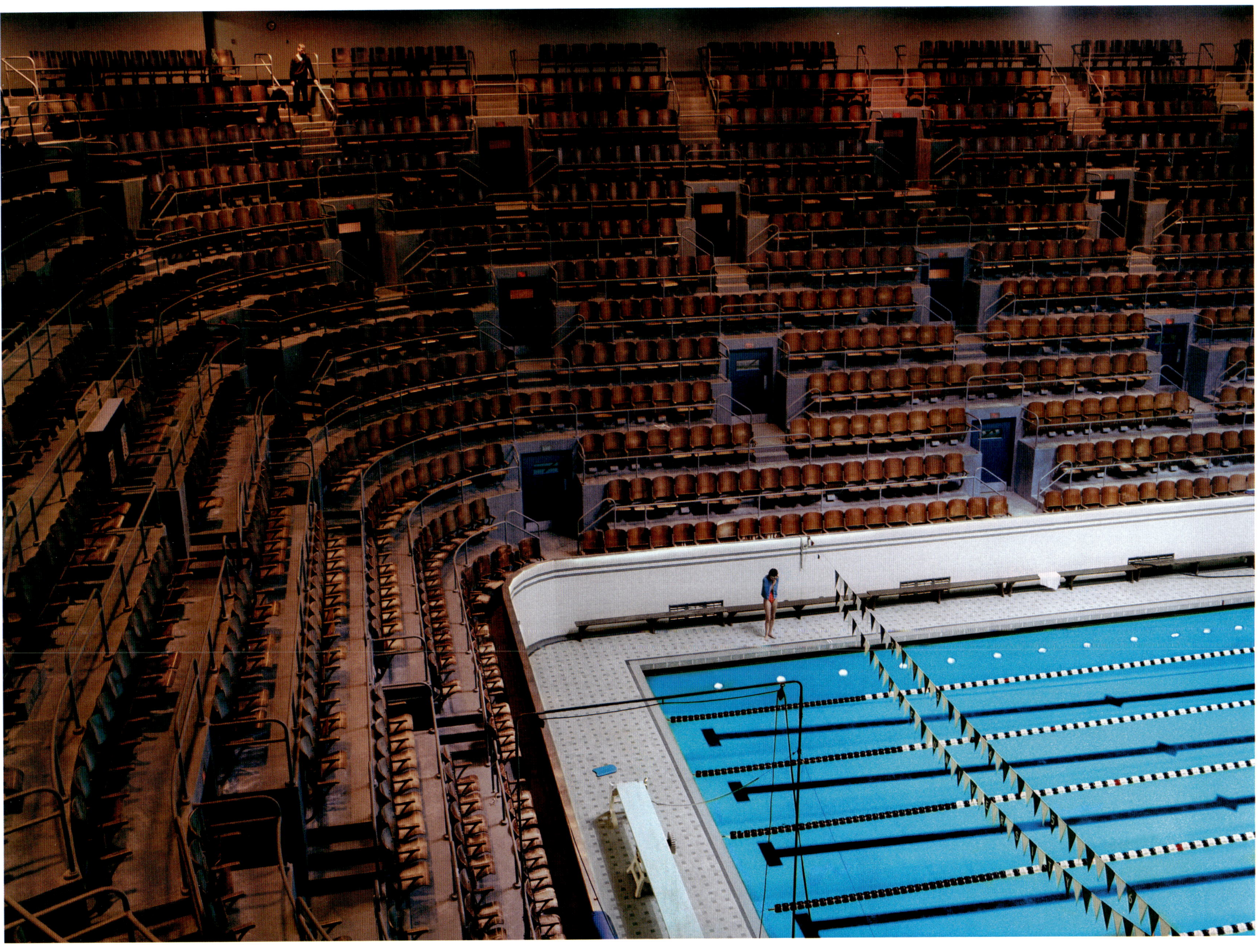

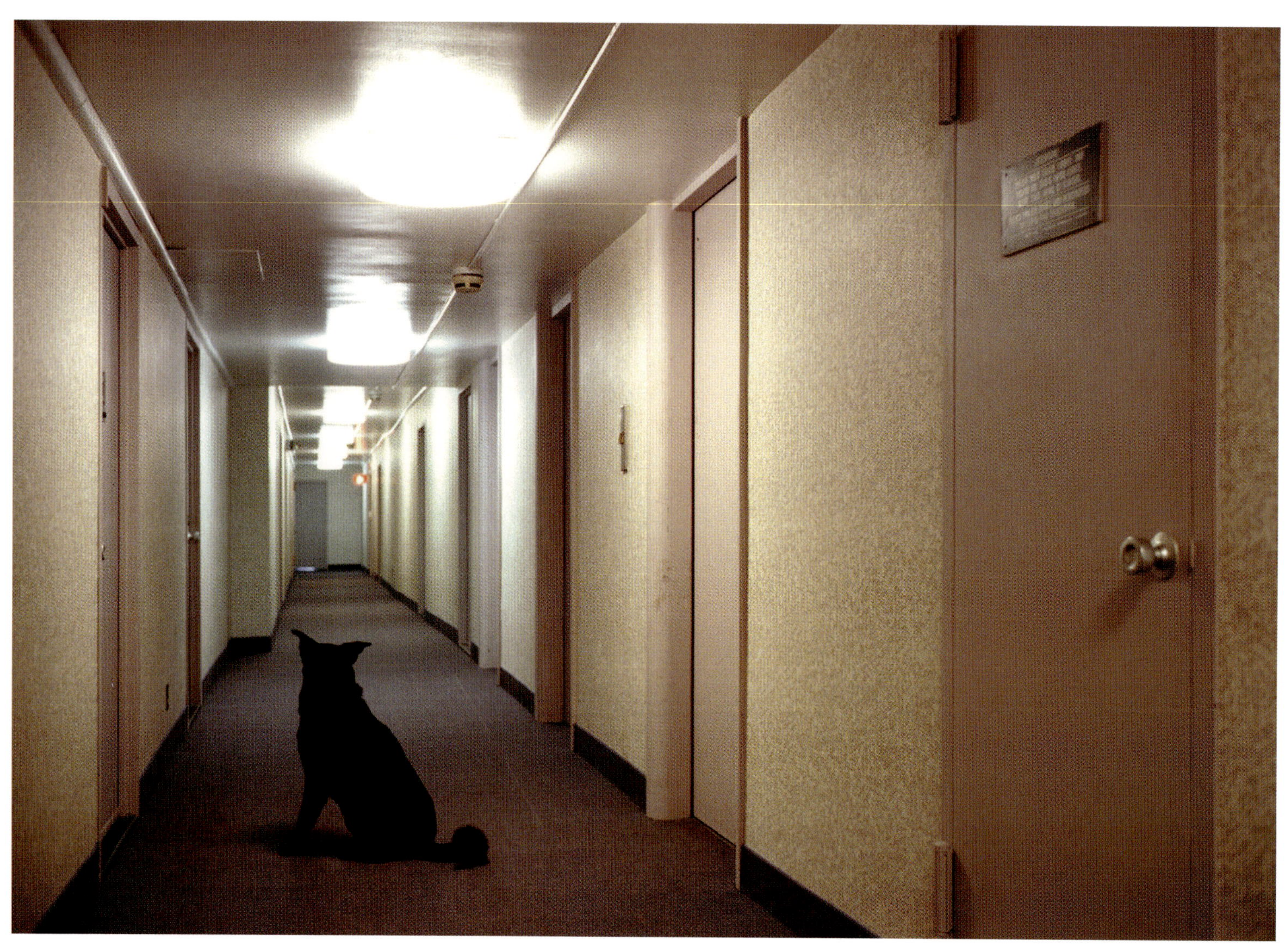

32 / Dog

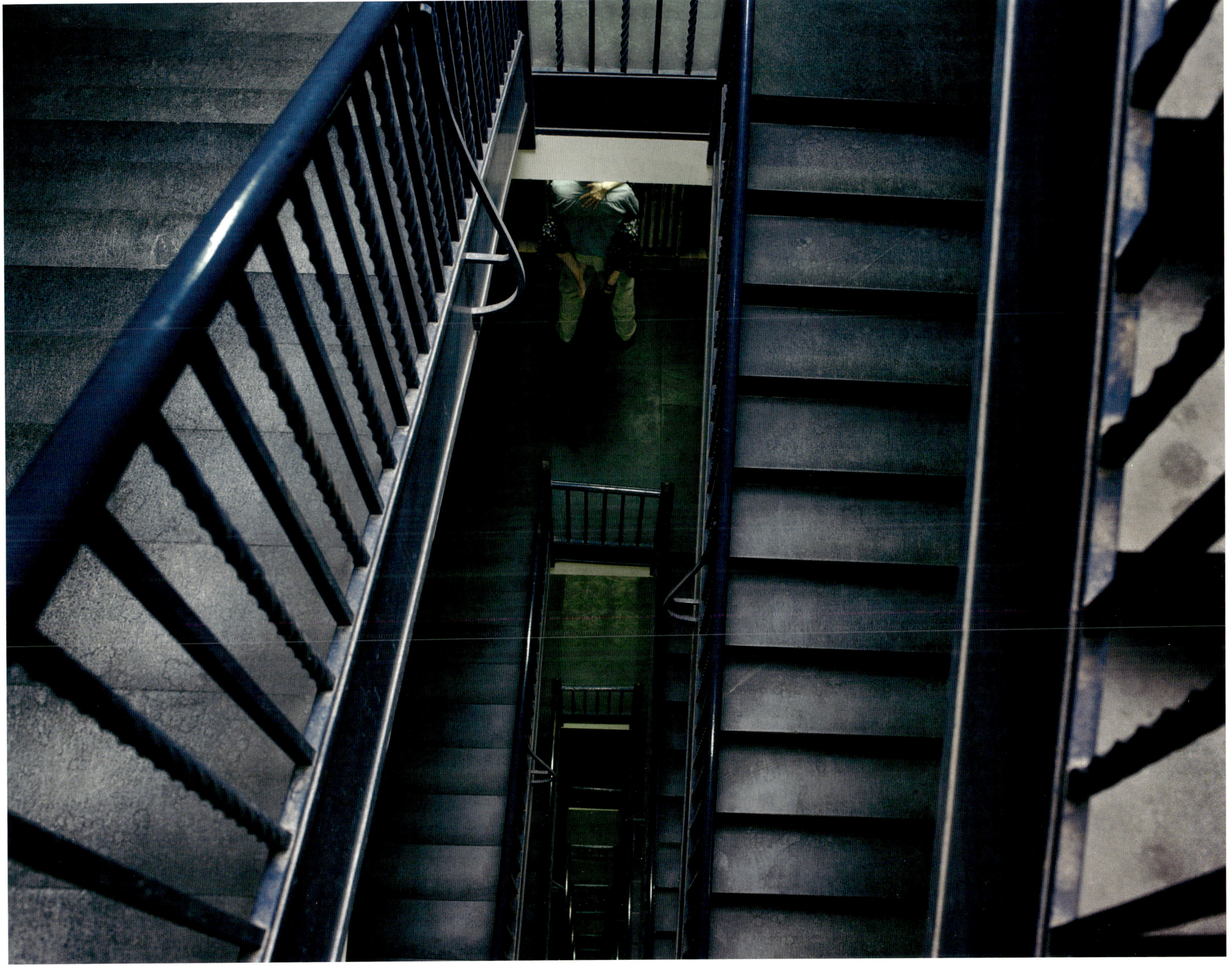

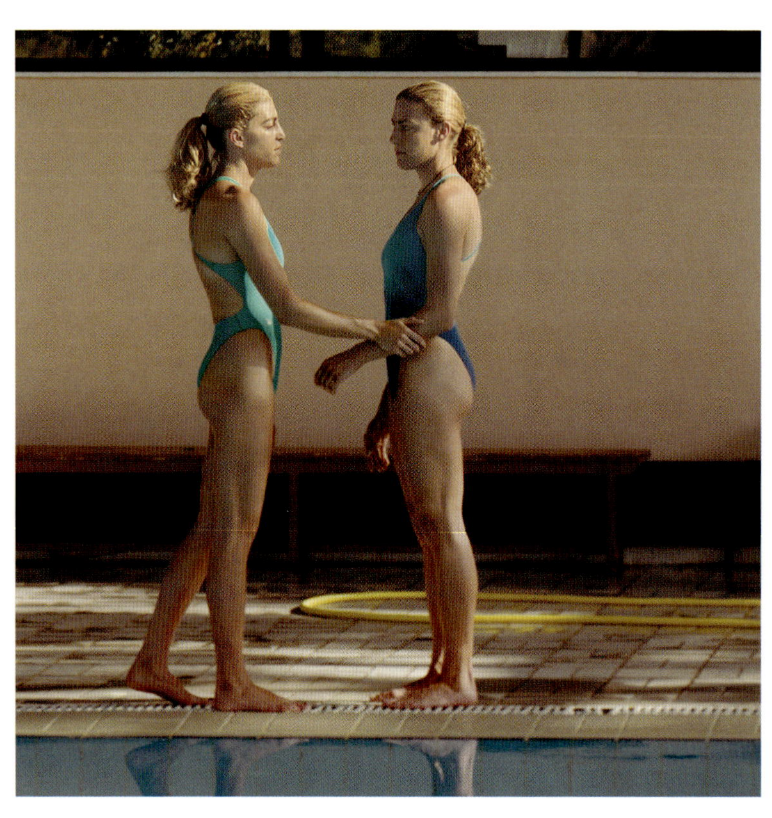

34 / Twins (detail)

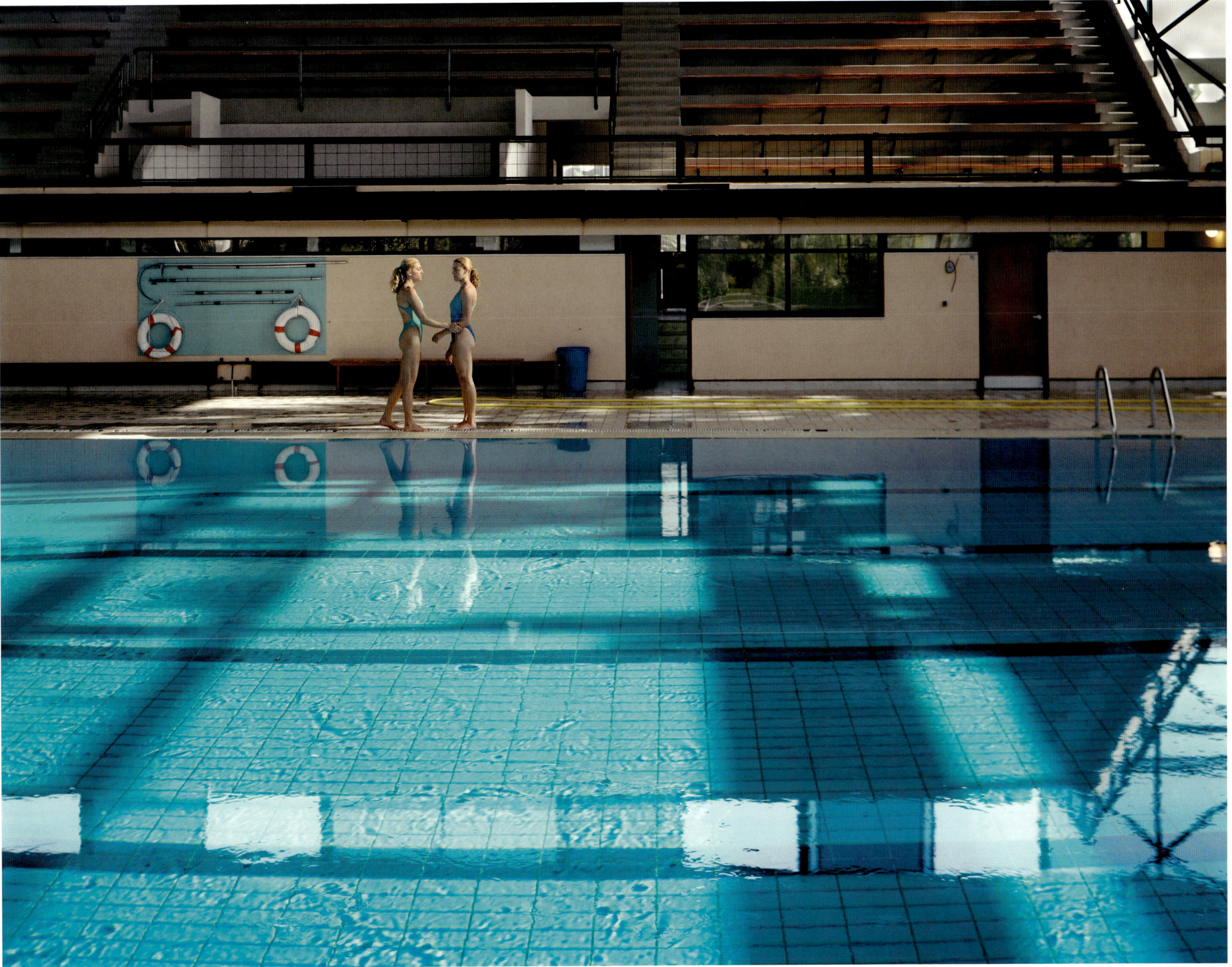

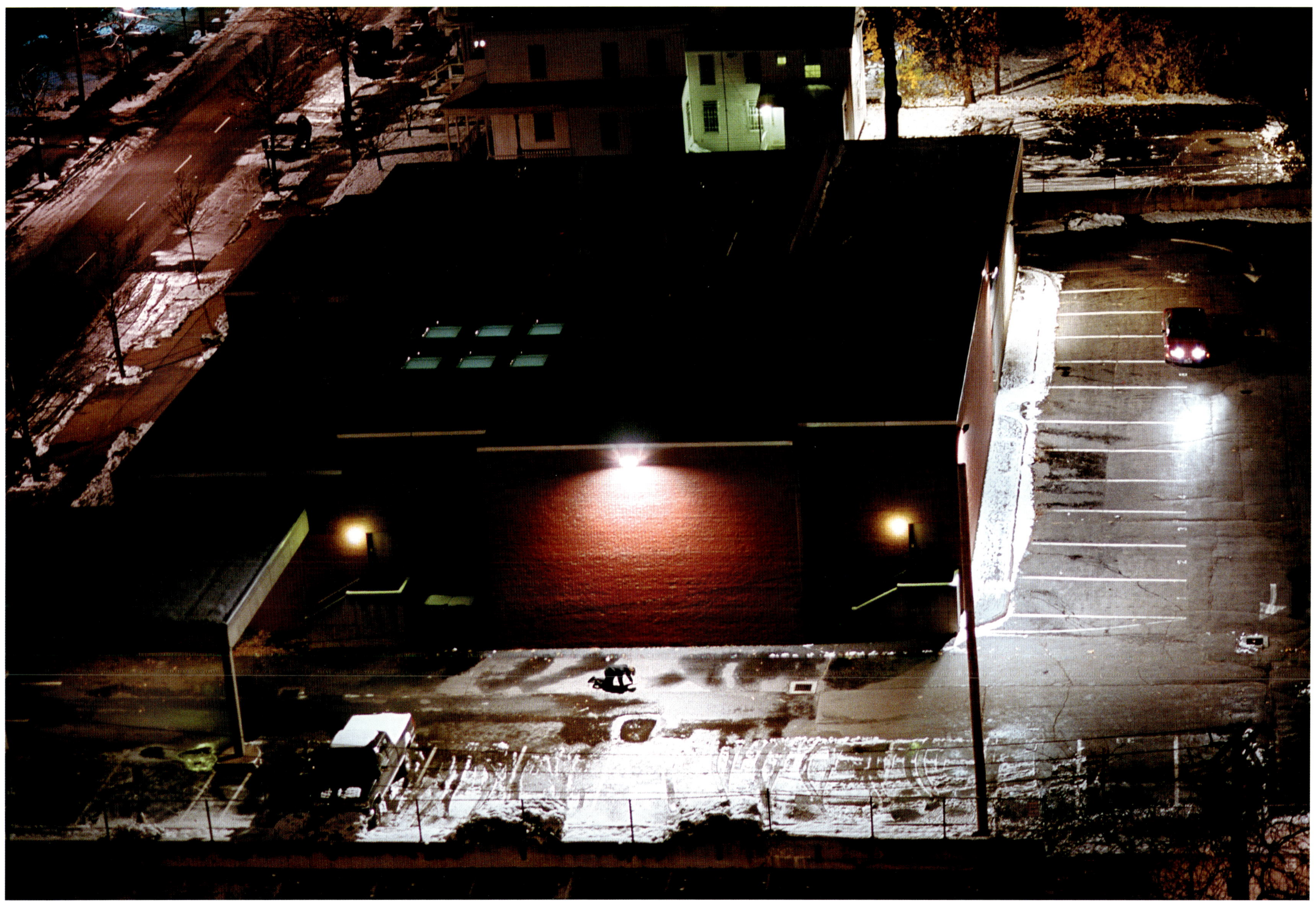

LANDSCAPES

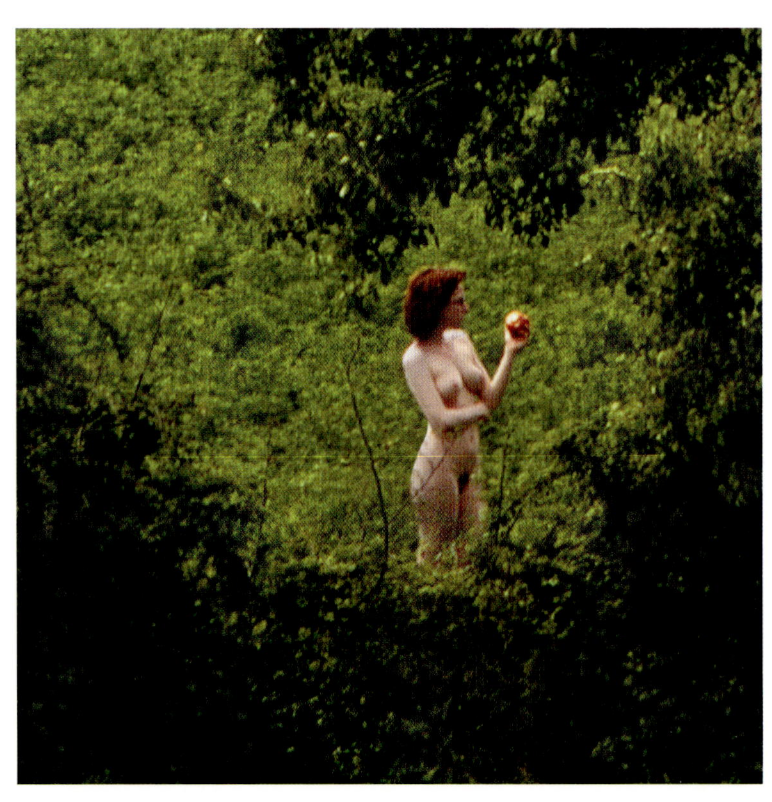

40 / Megla (detail)

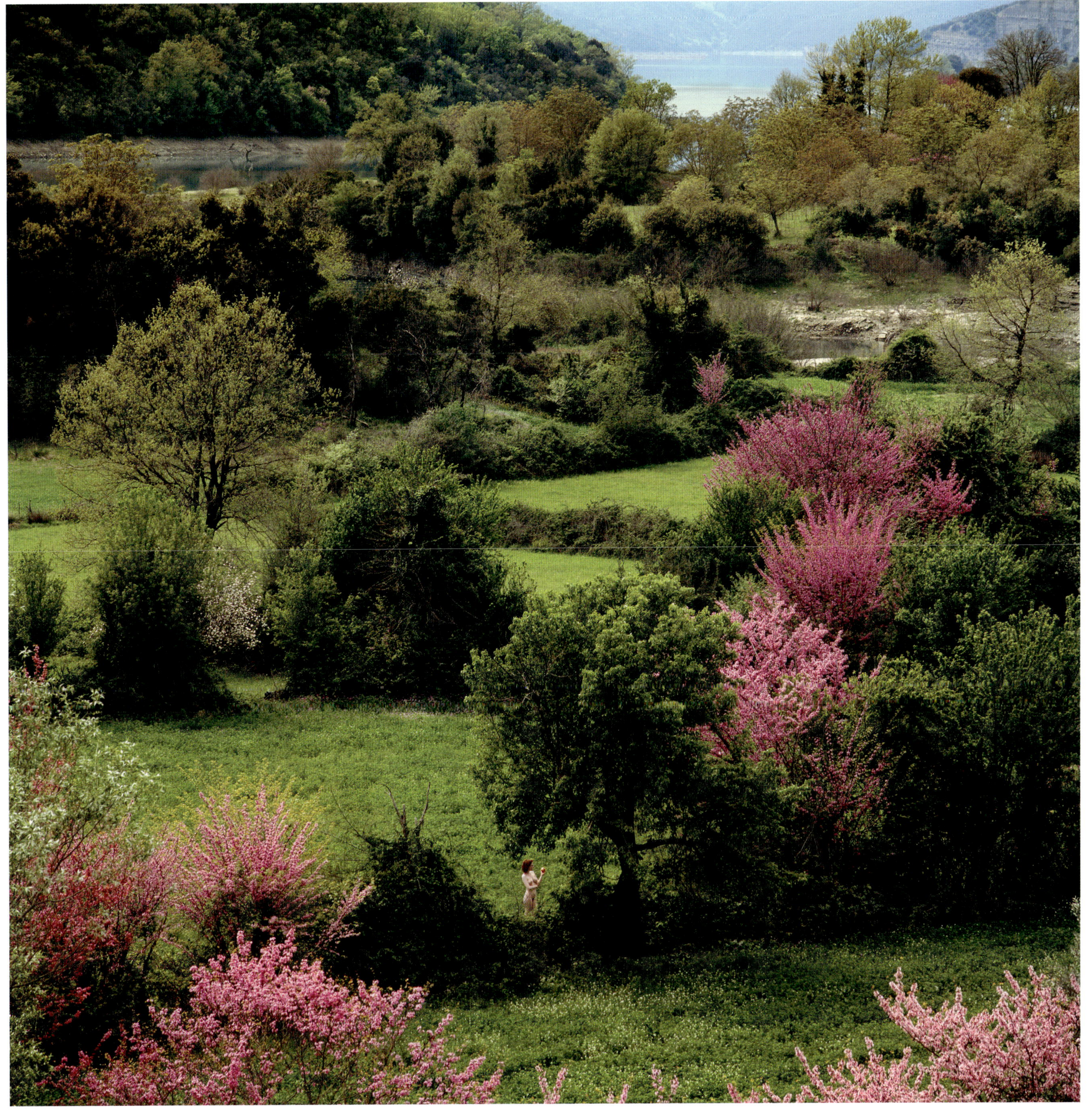

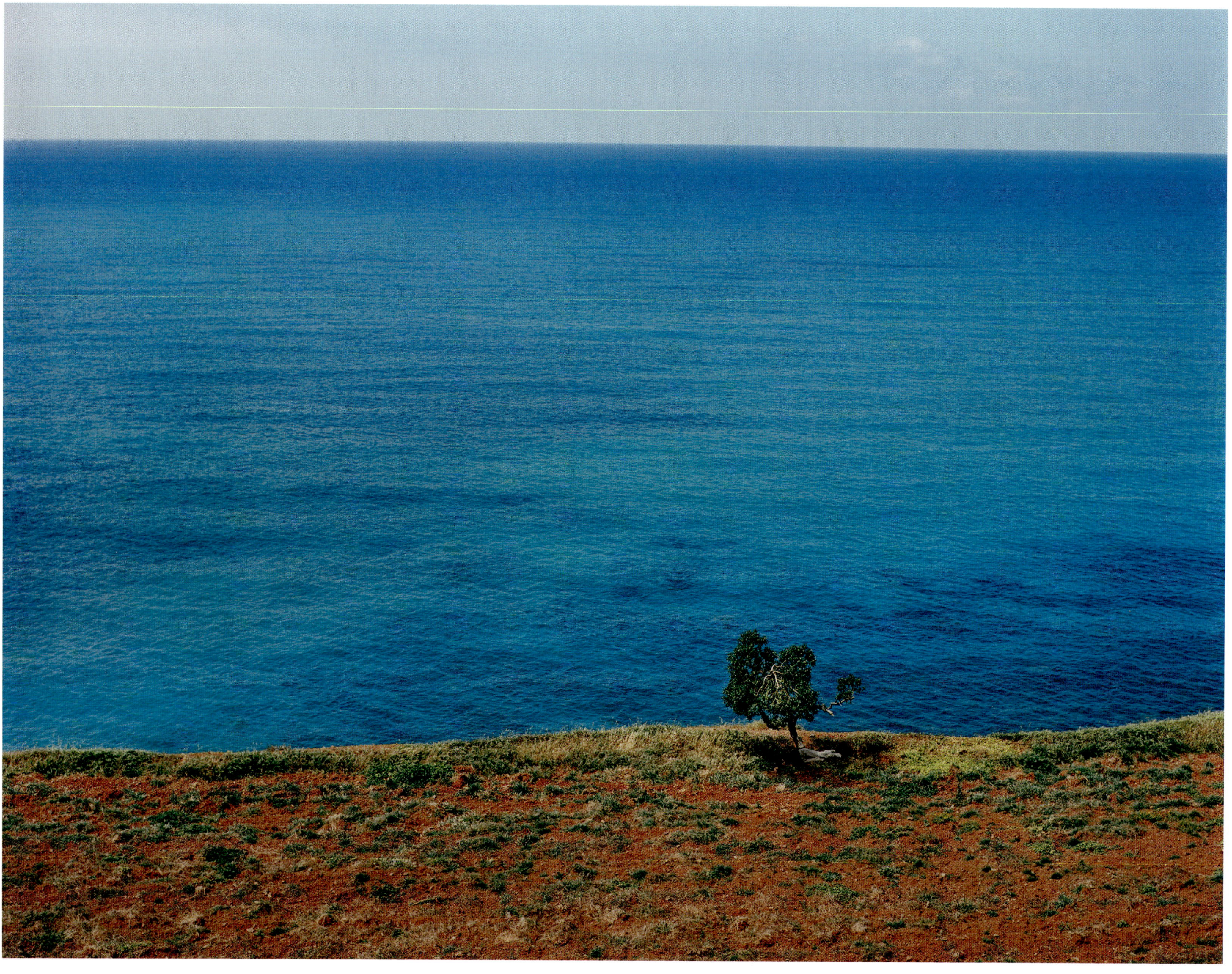

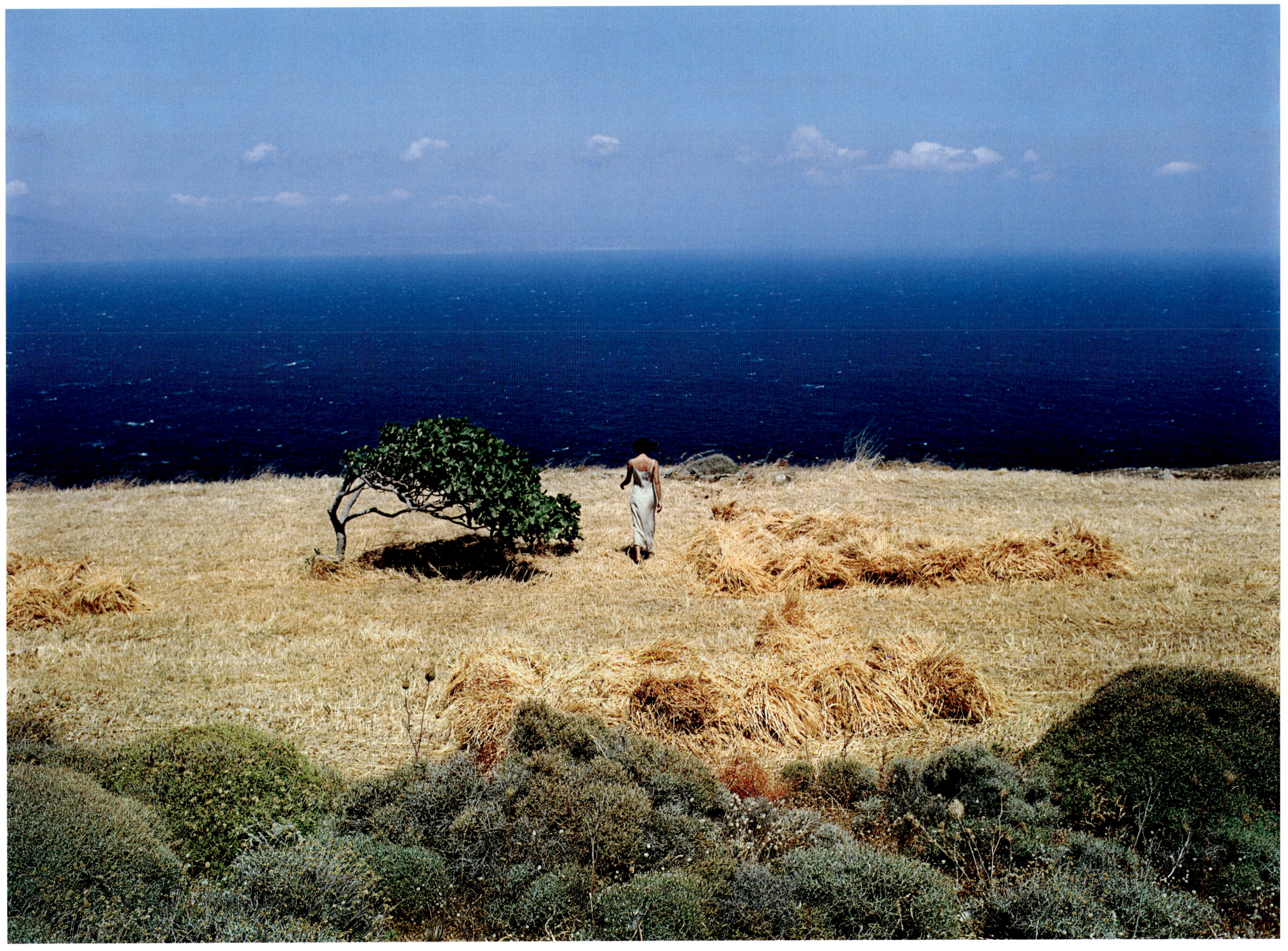

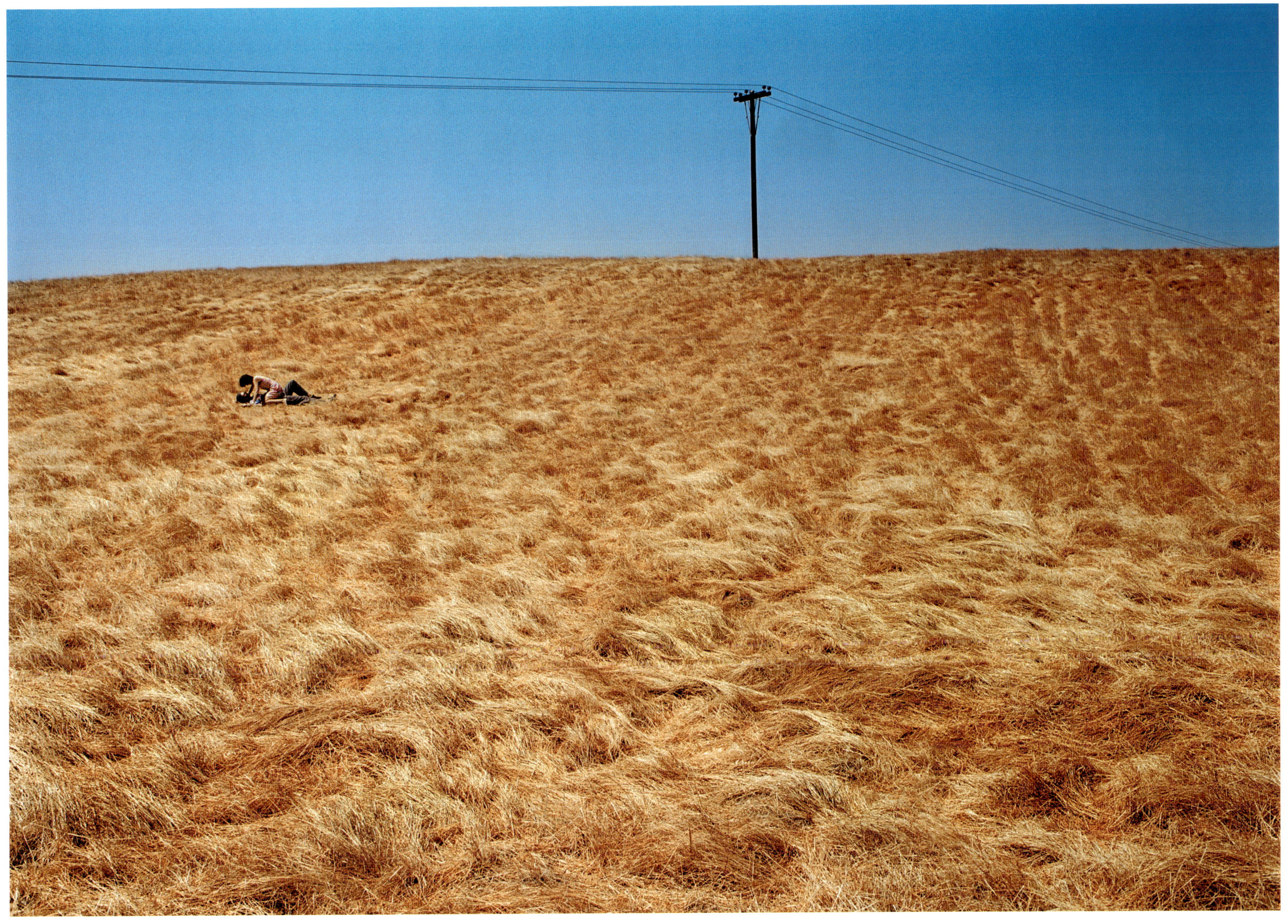

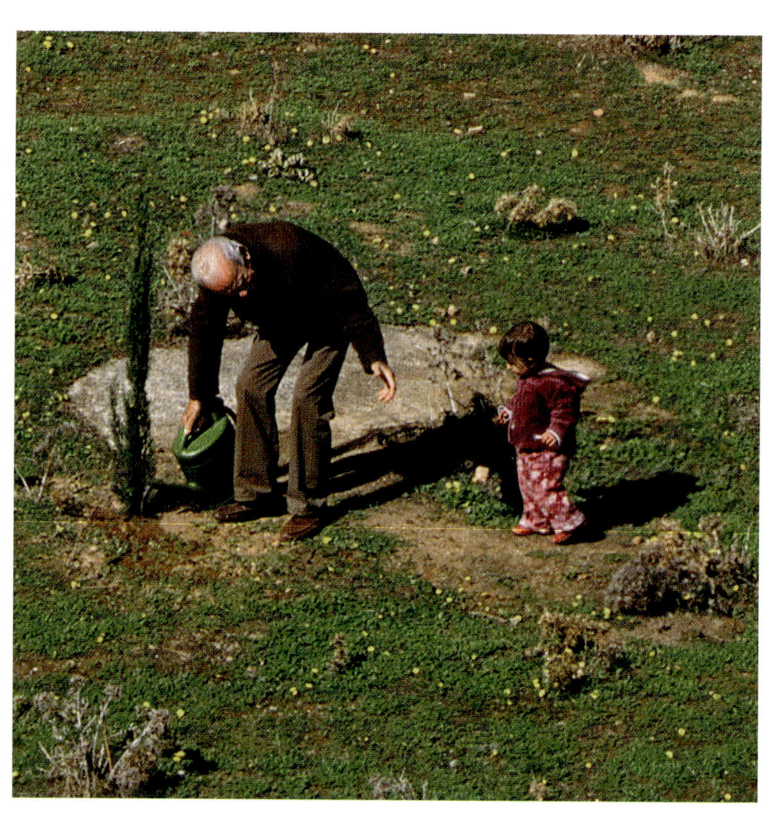

46 / Circle (detail)

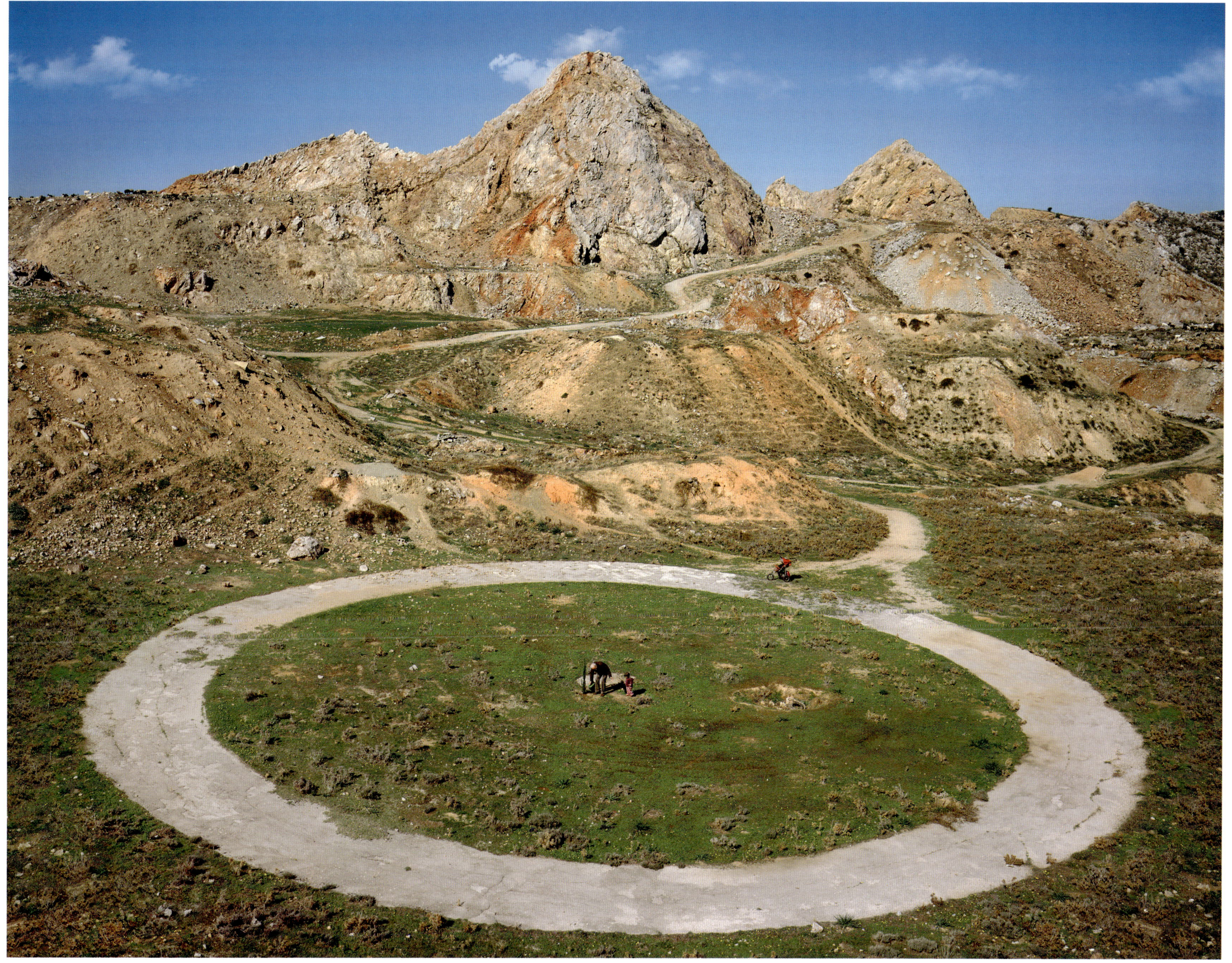

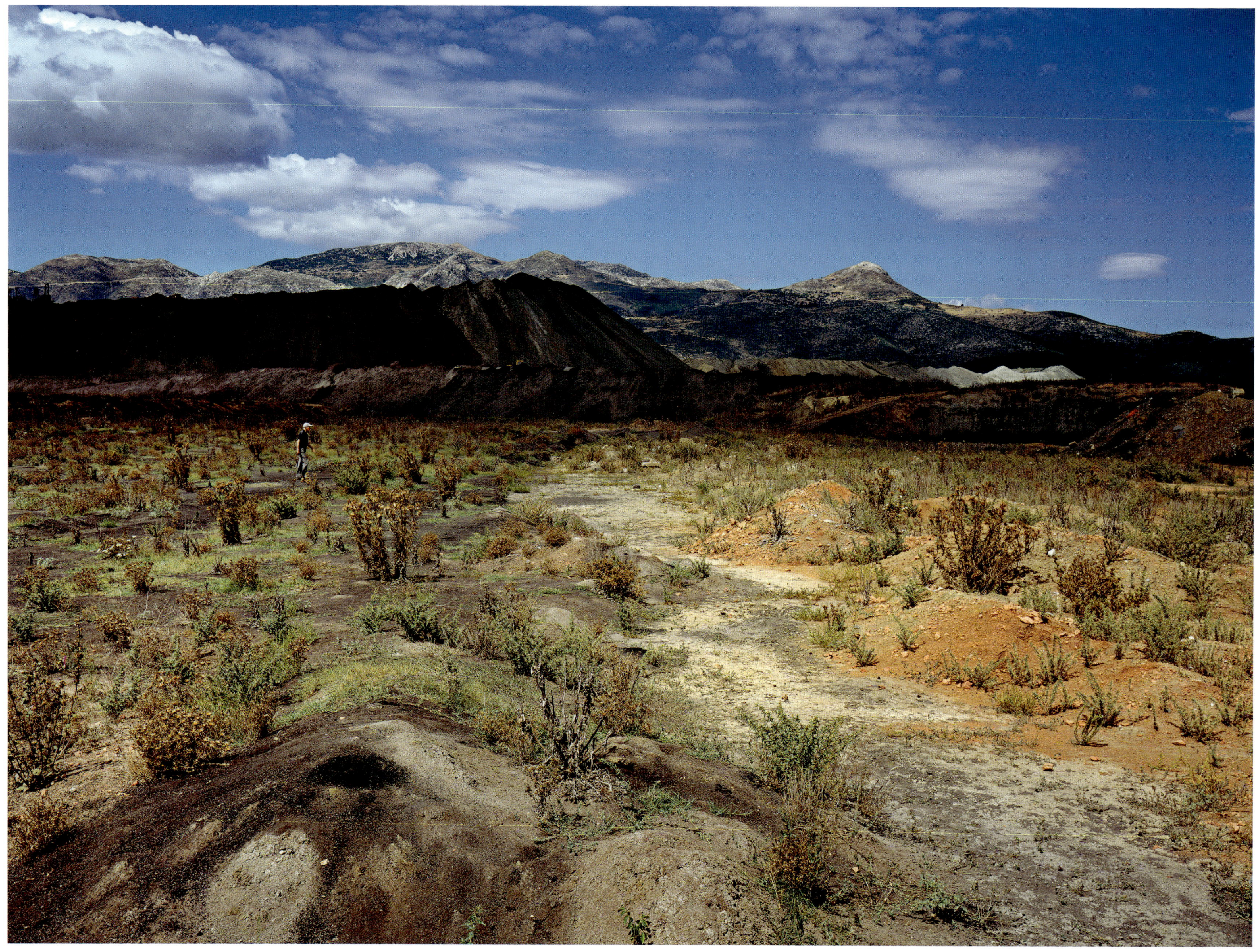

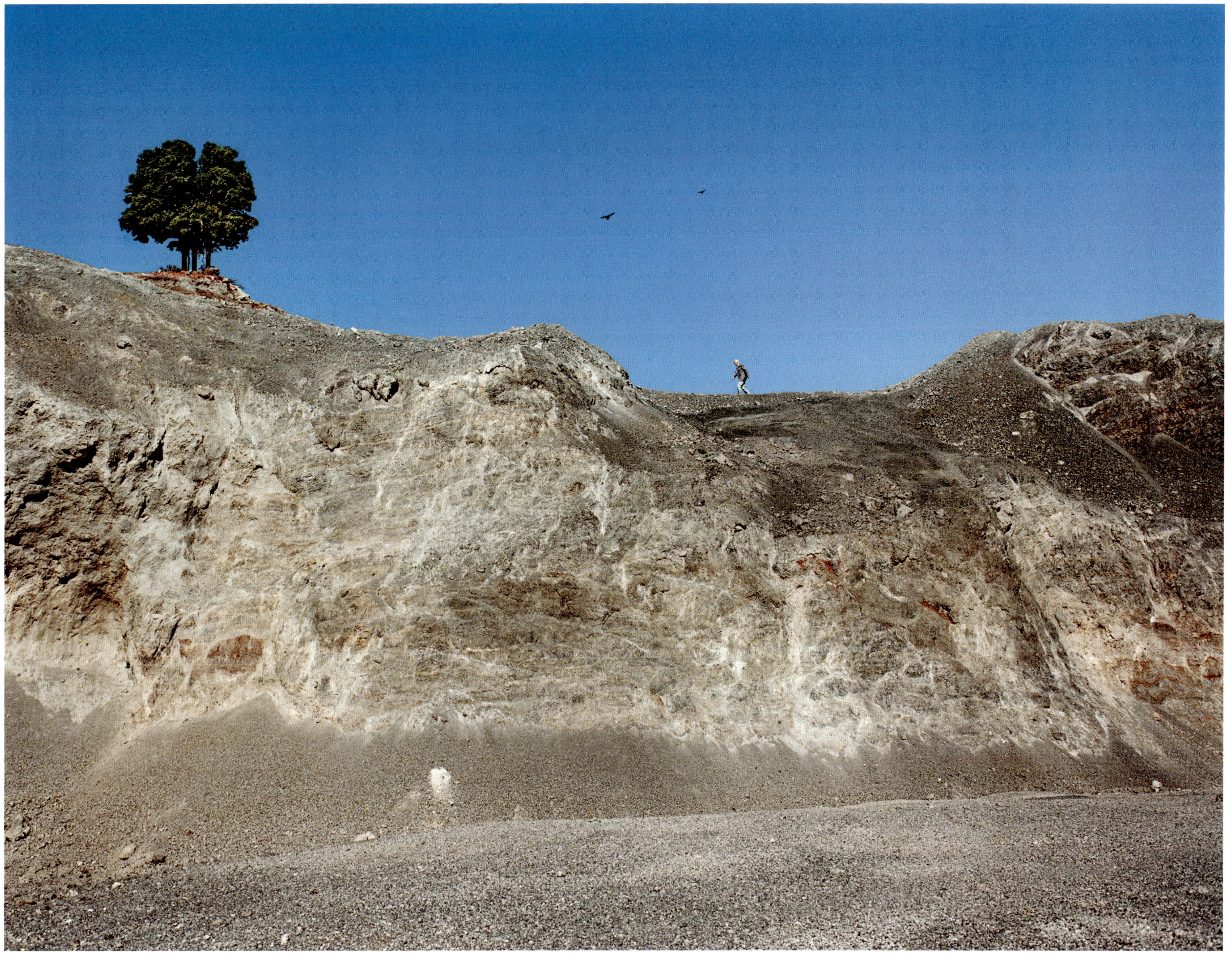

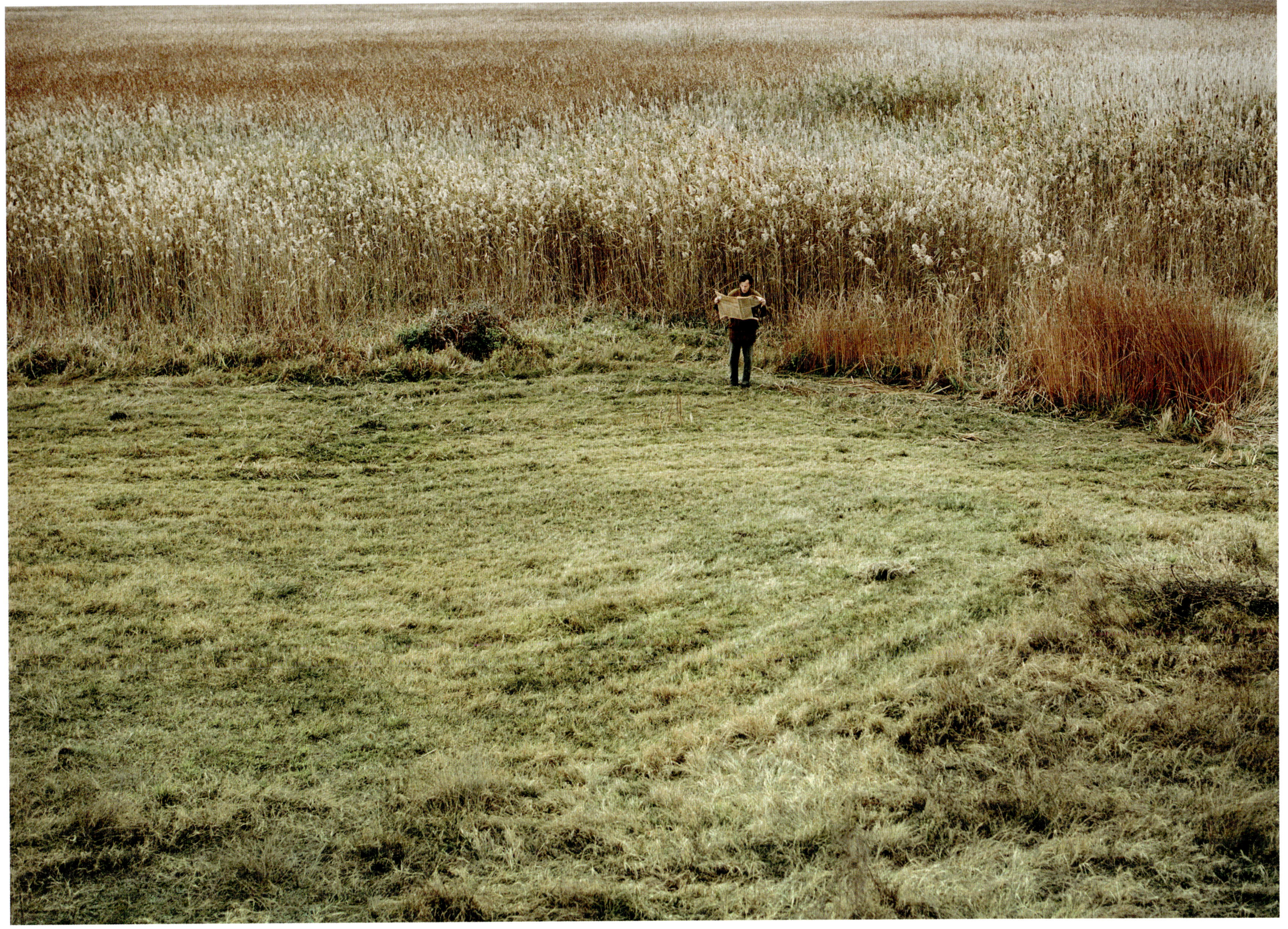

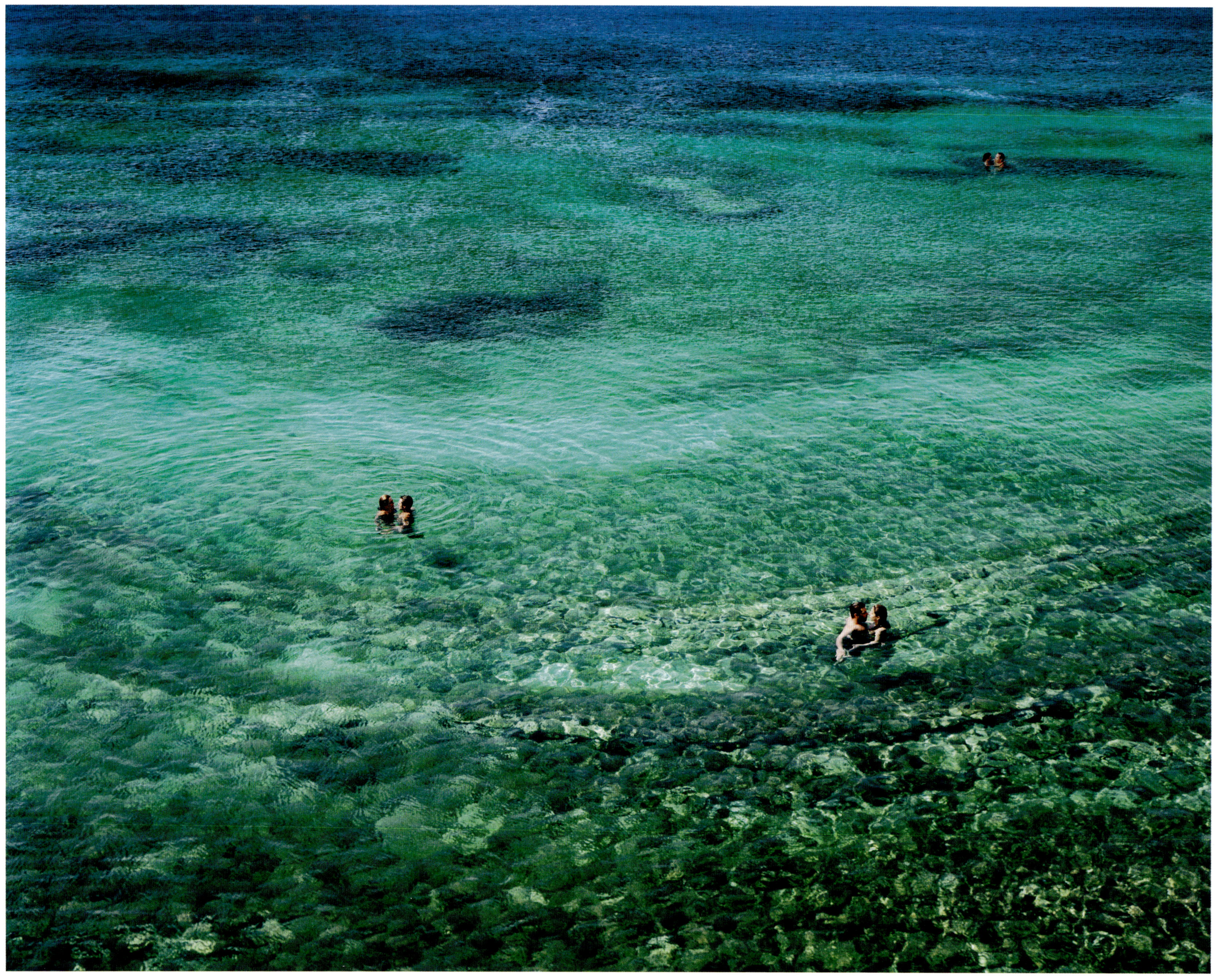

52 / Aghida

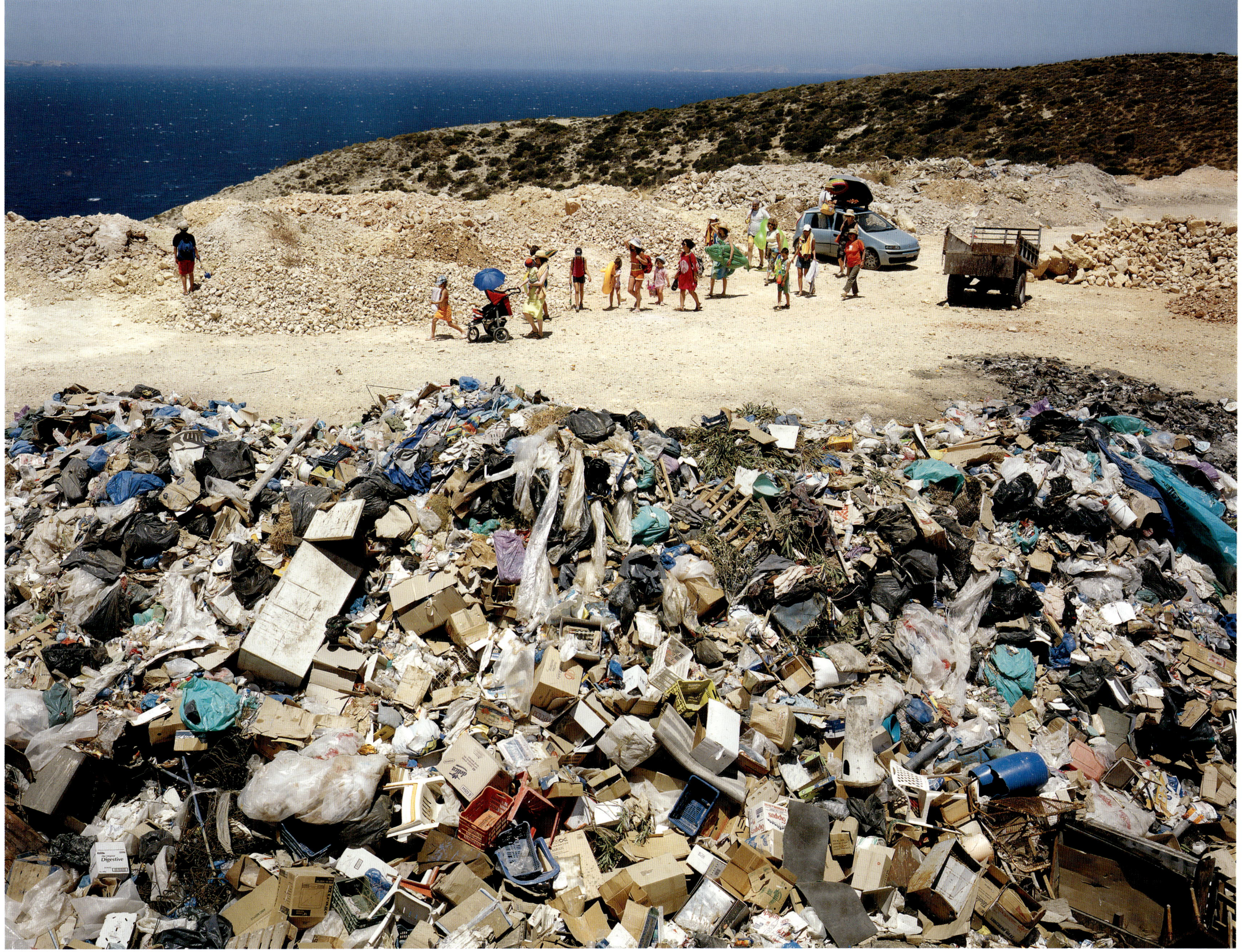

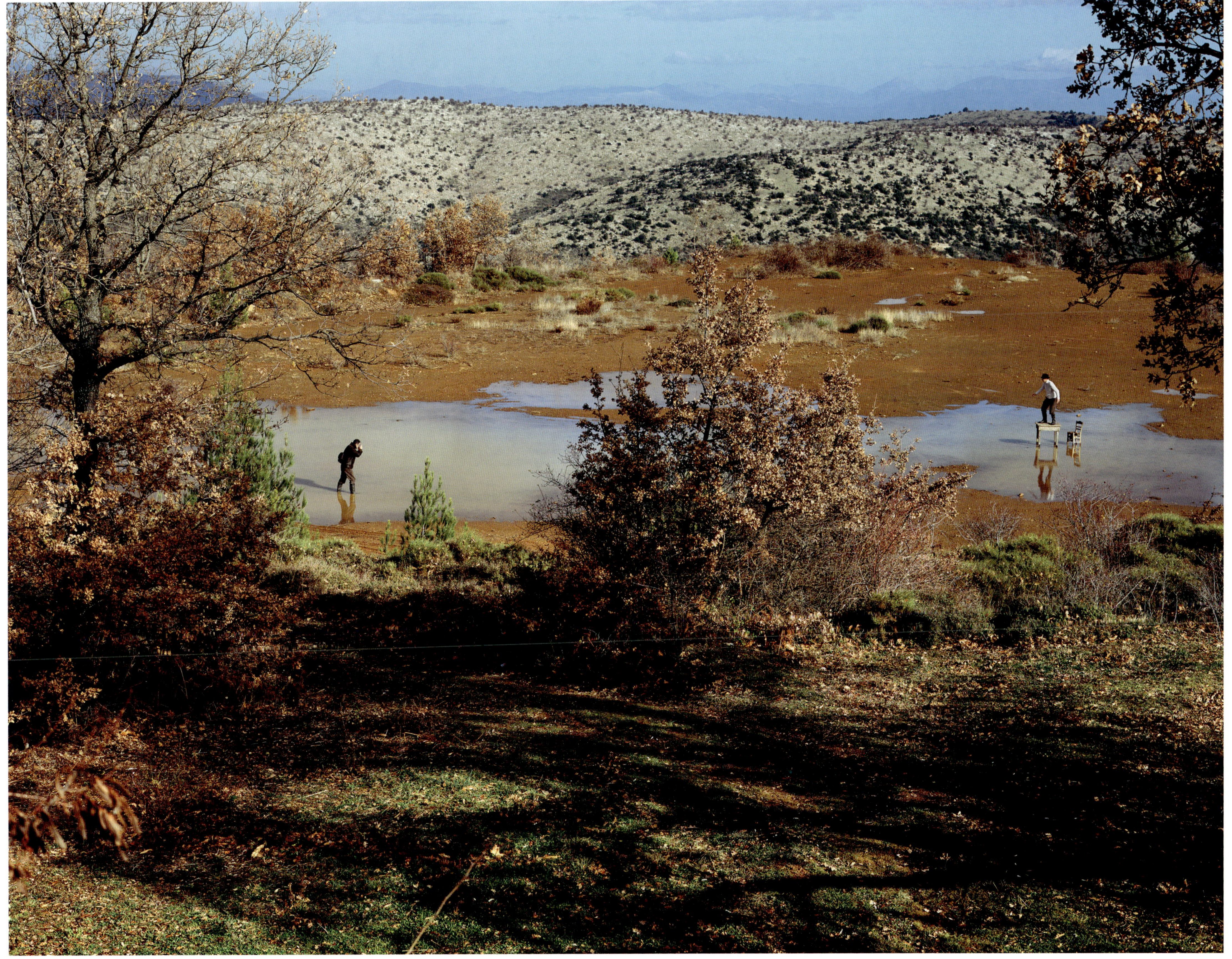

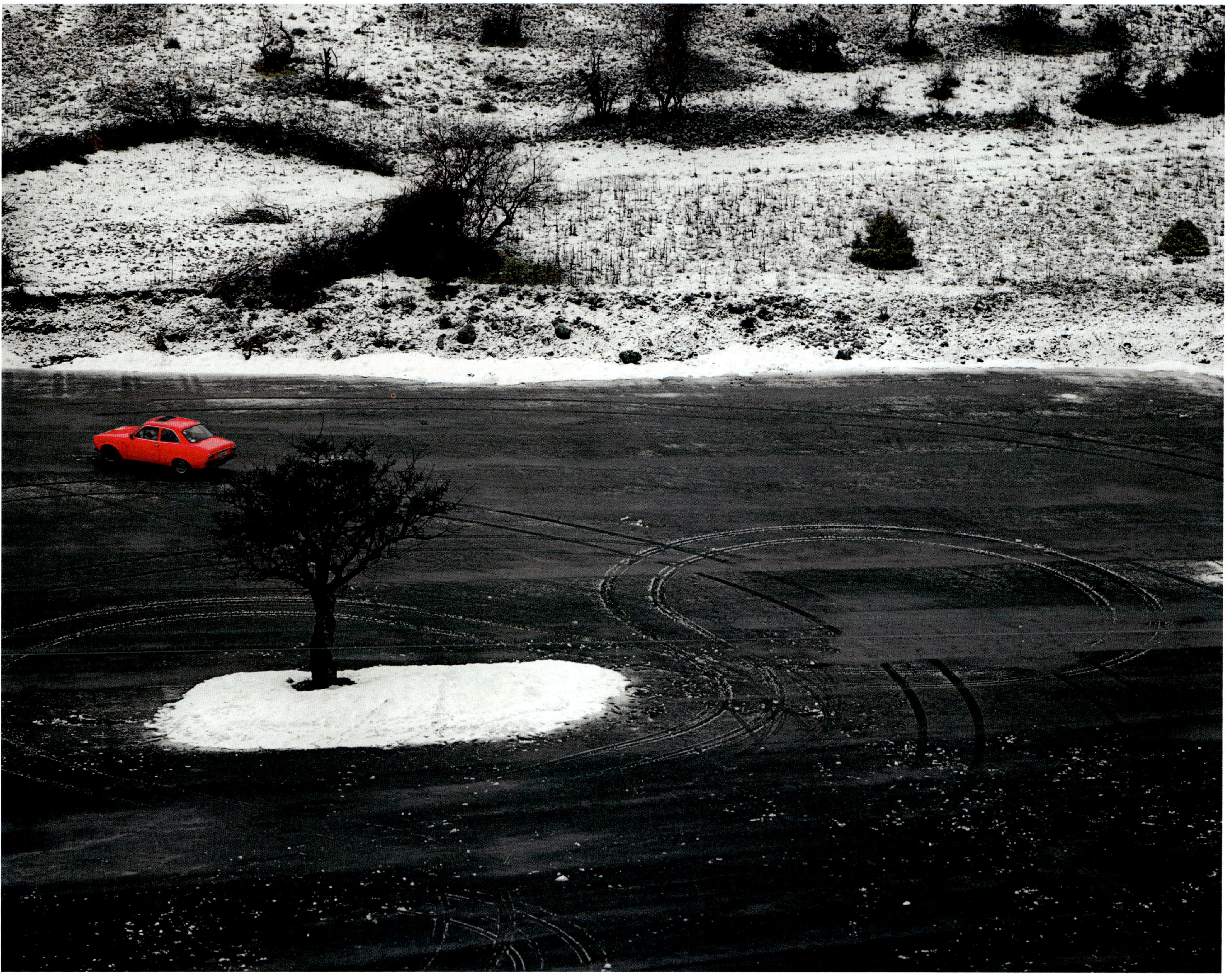

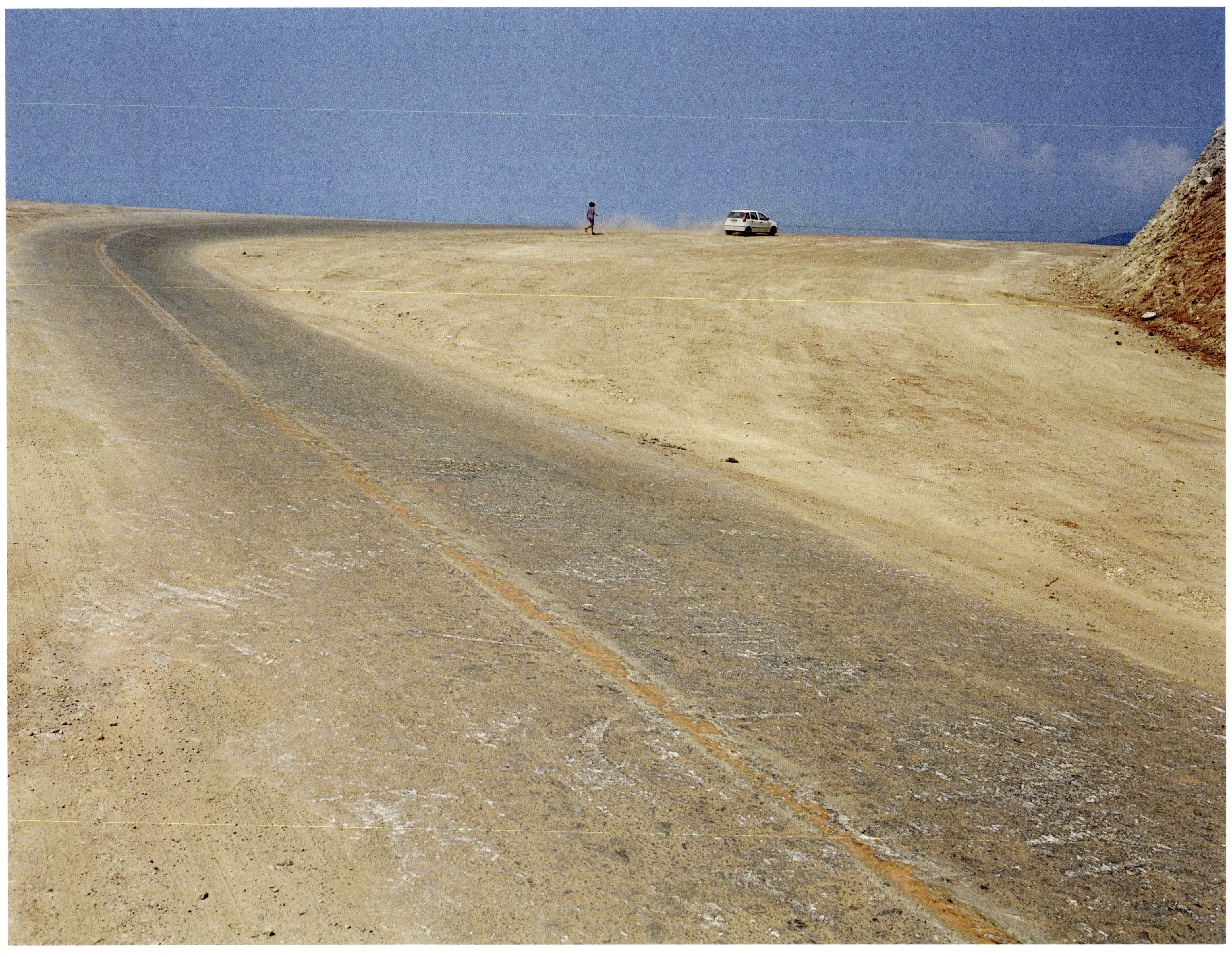

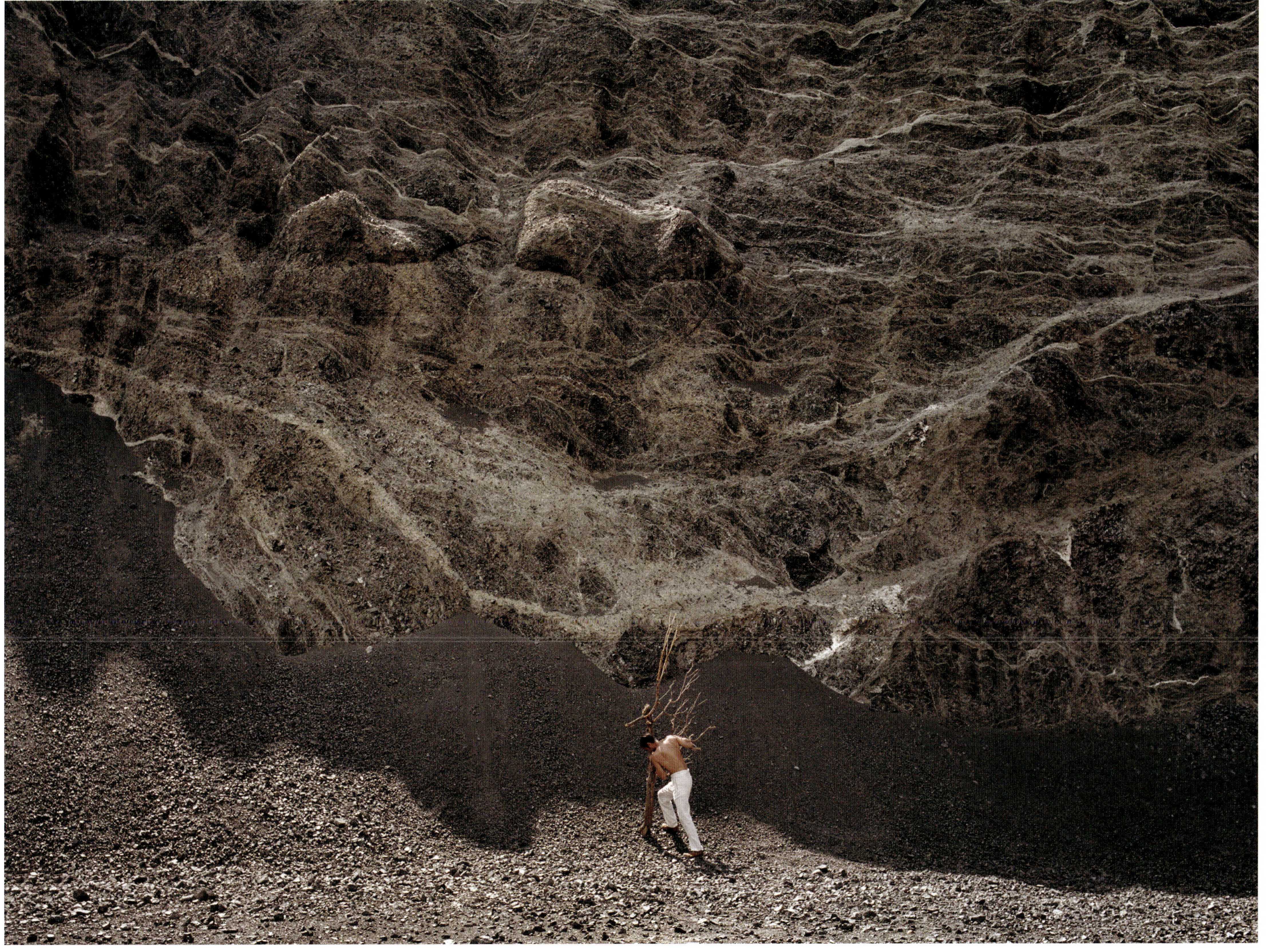

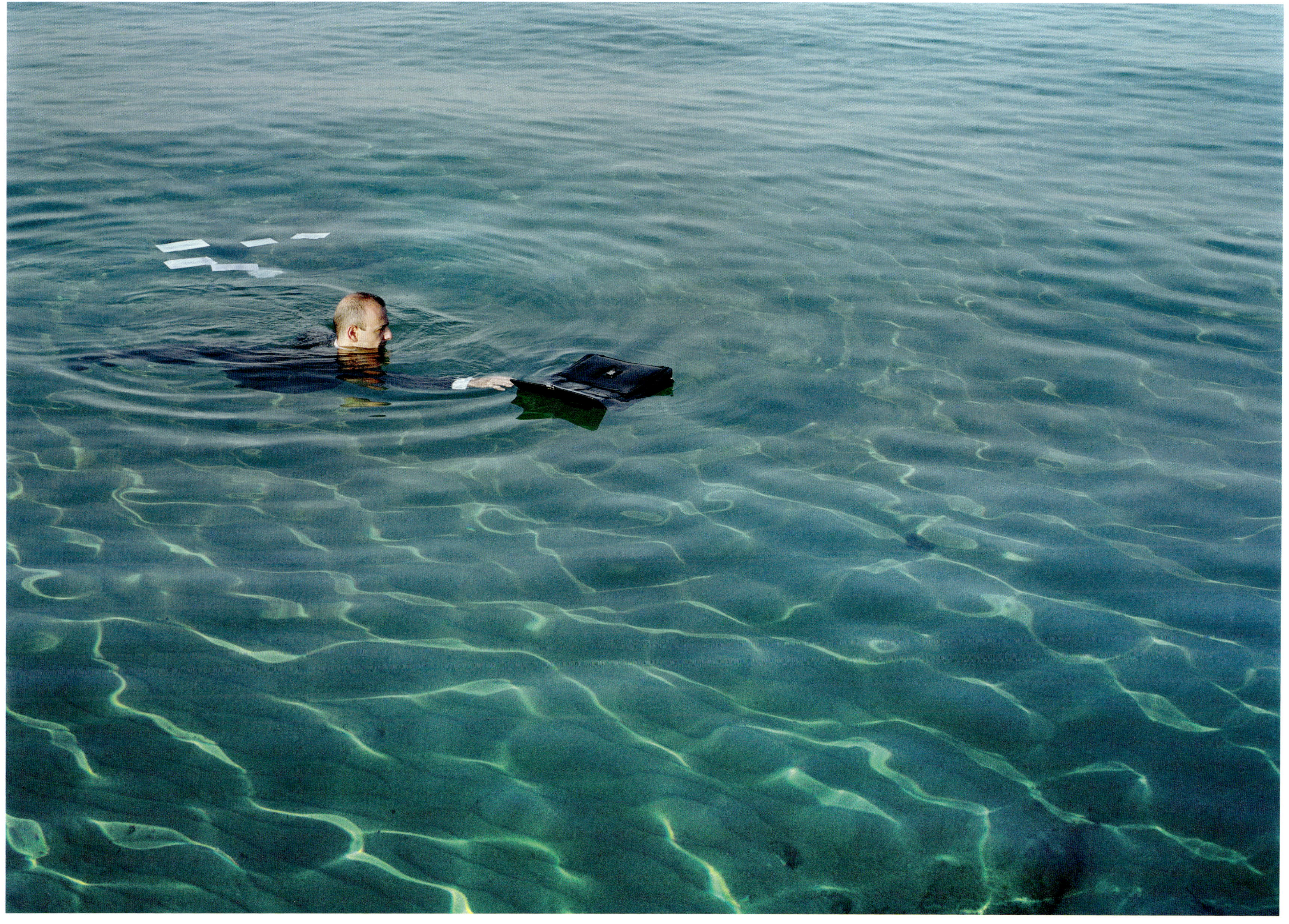

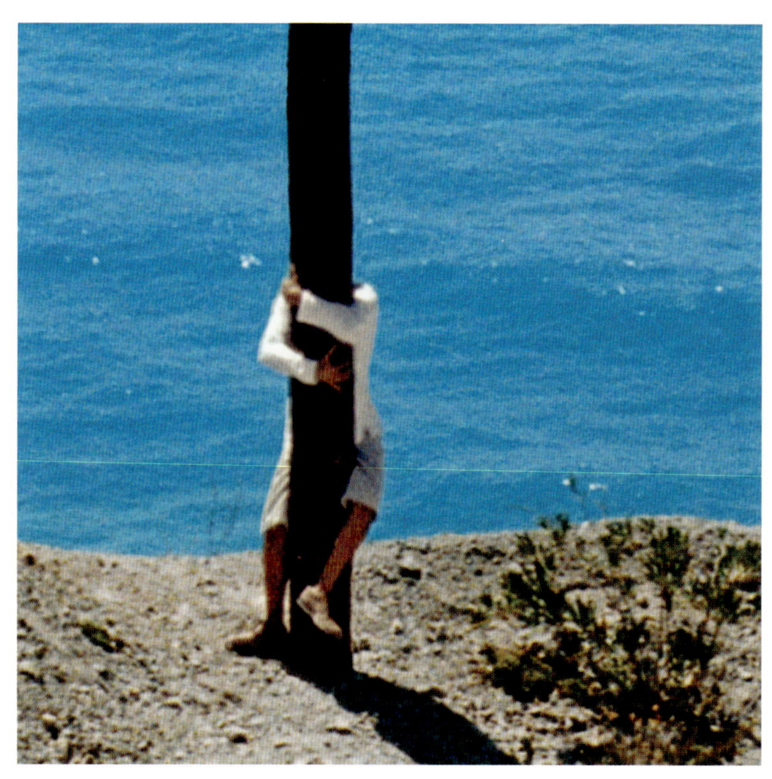

62 / Kremasmata (detail)

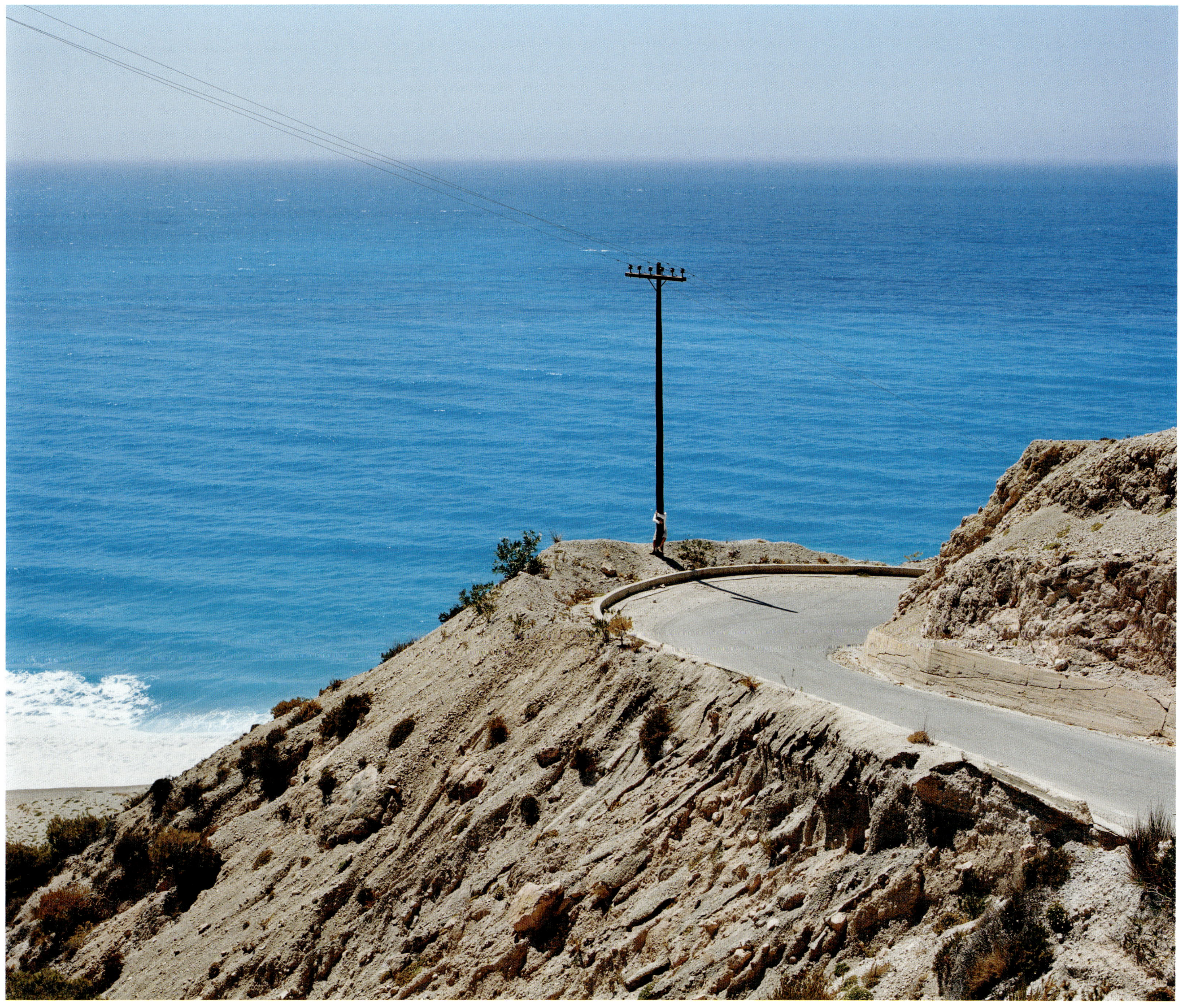

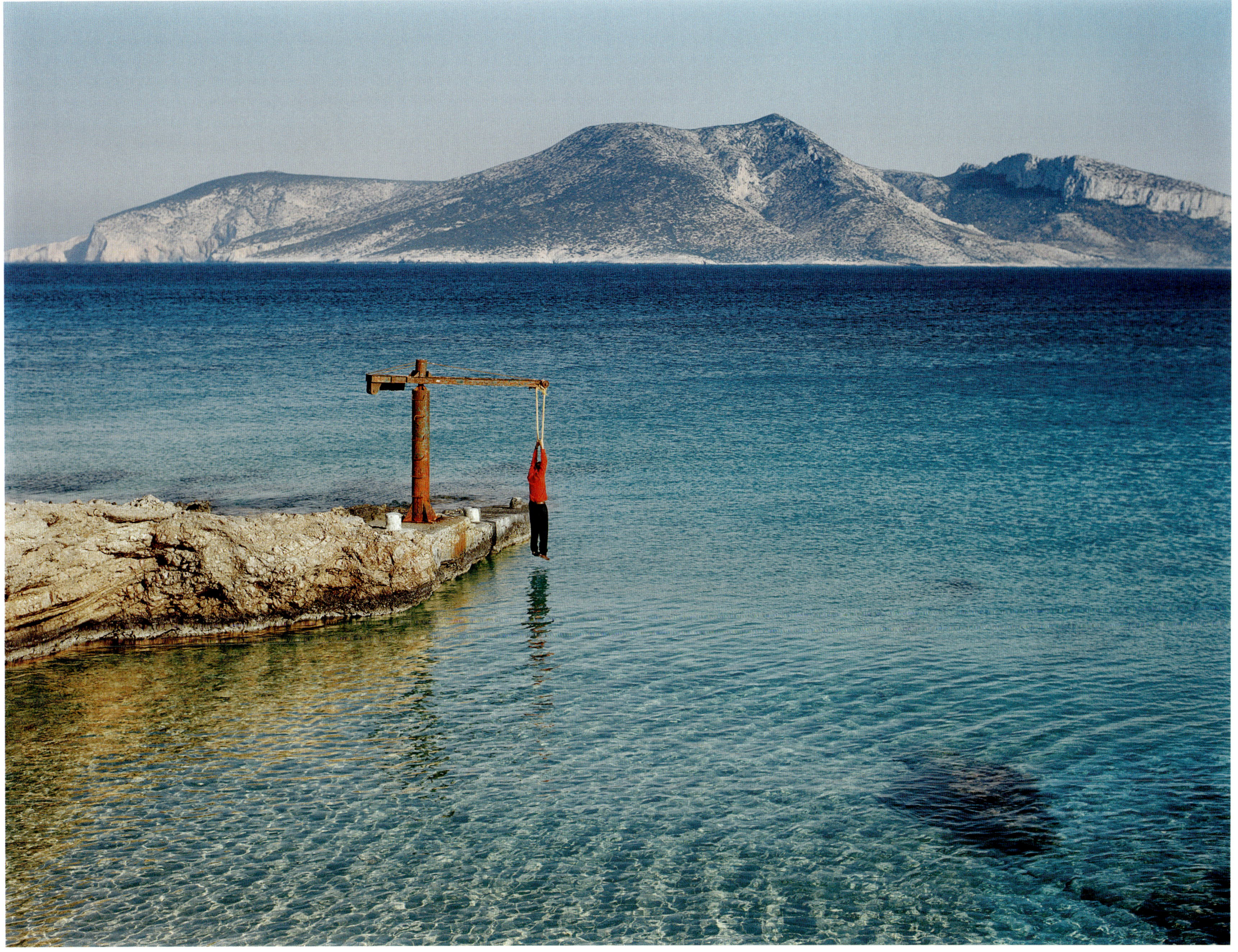

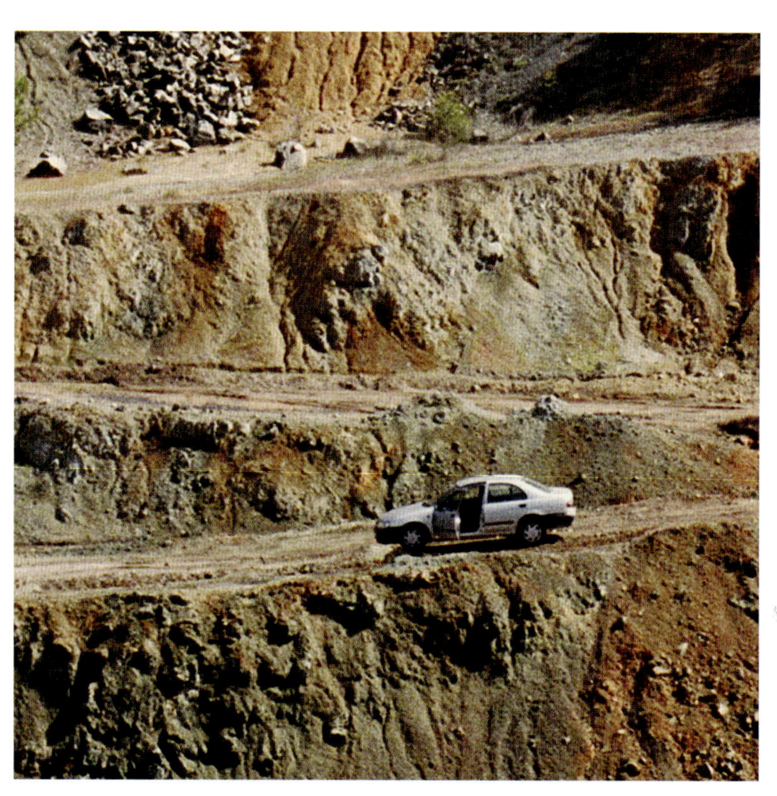

66 / Mitsero (detail)

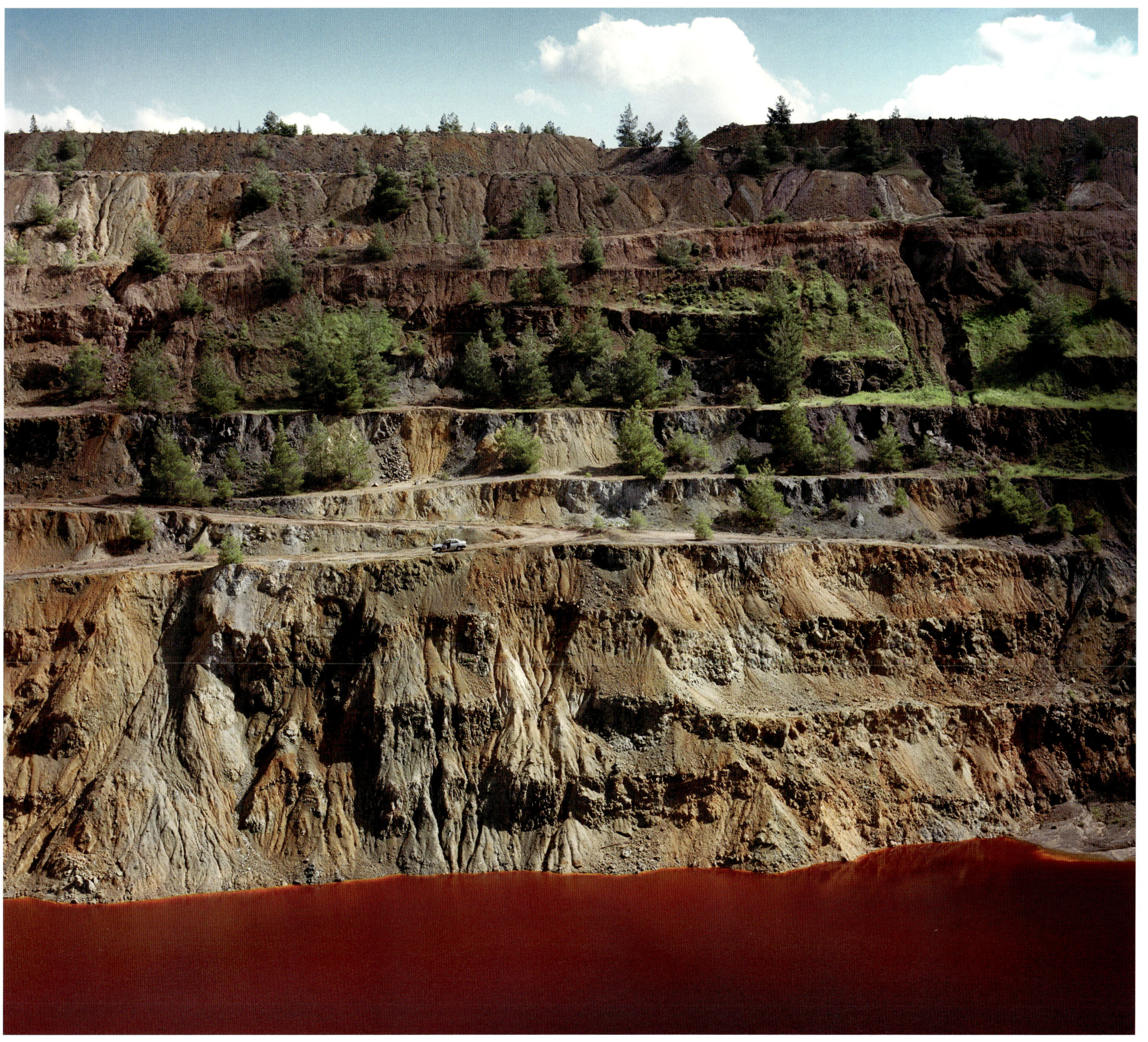

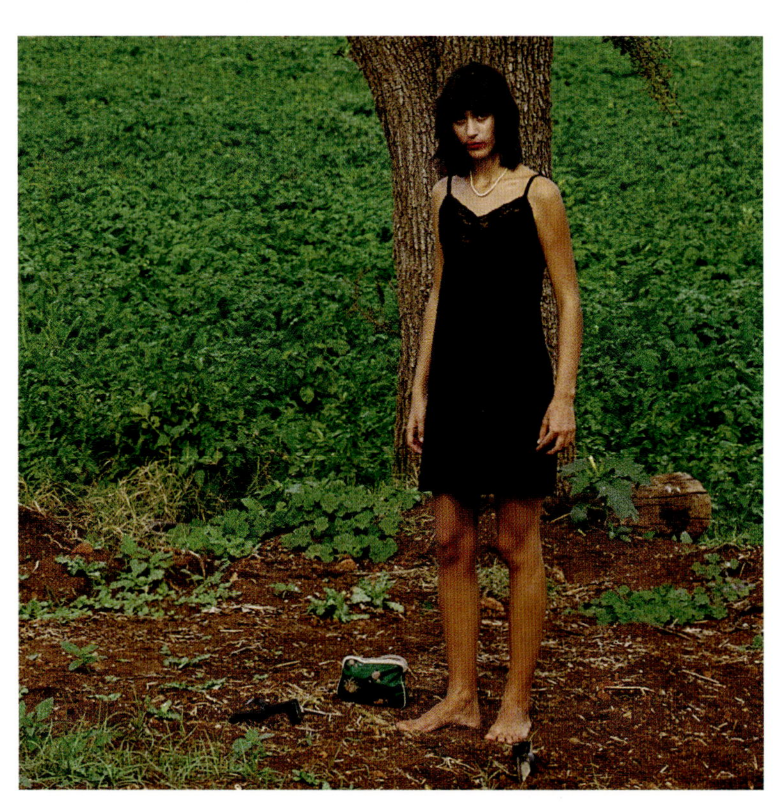

68 / Ypato (detail)

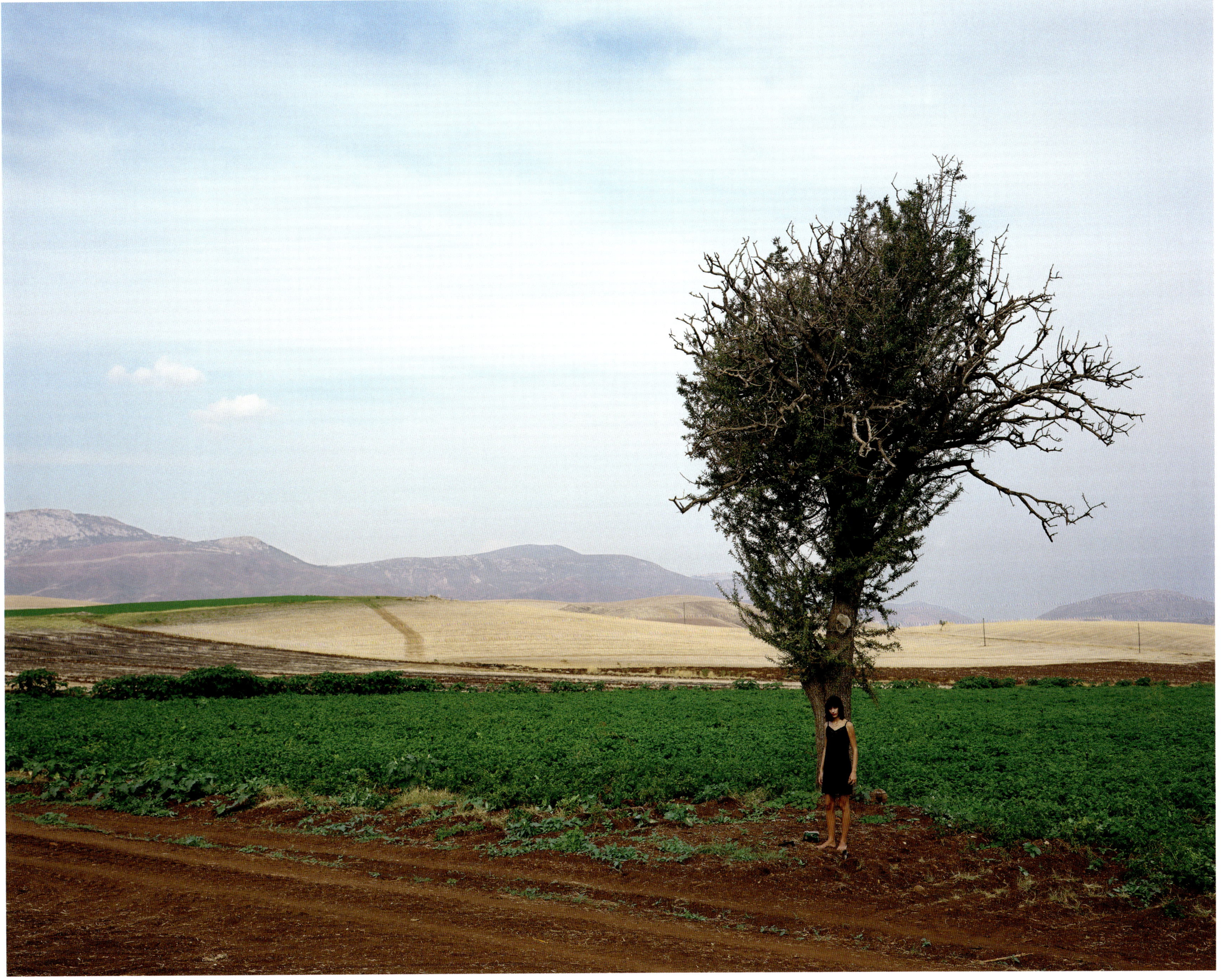

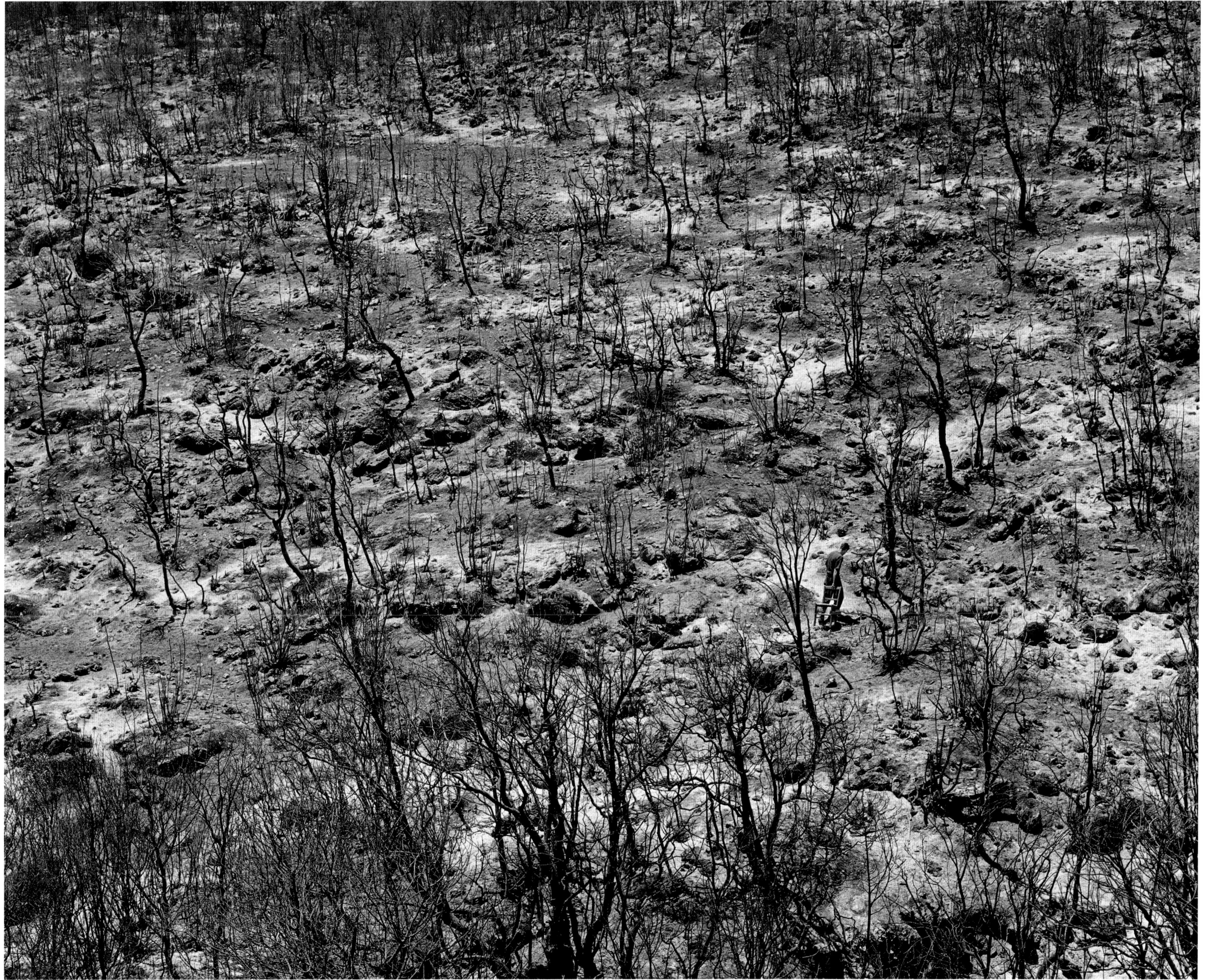

HERE WE ARE

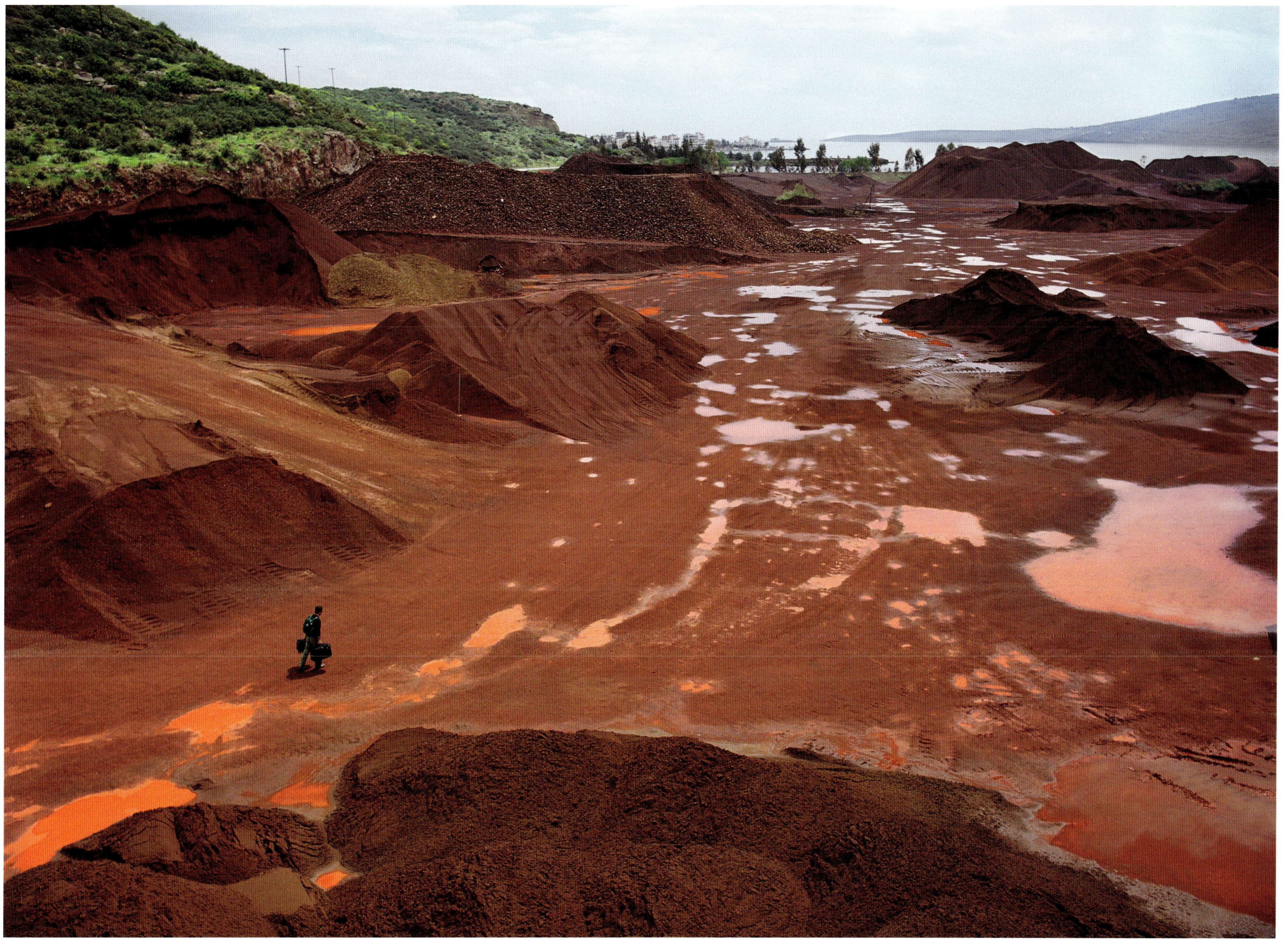

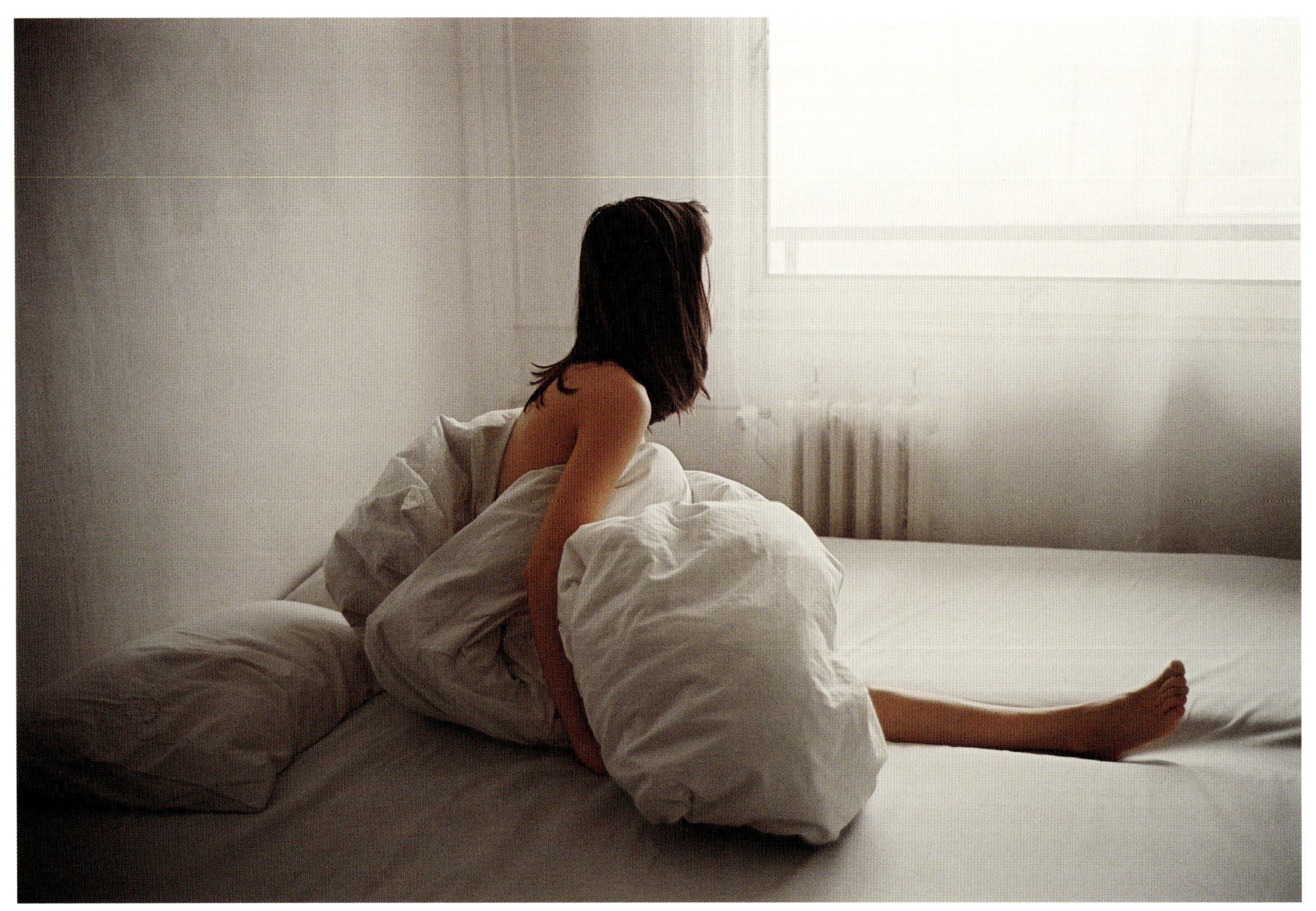

76 / Kyriaki

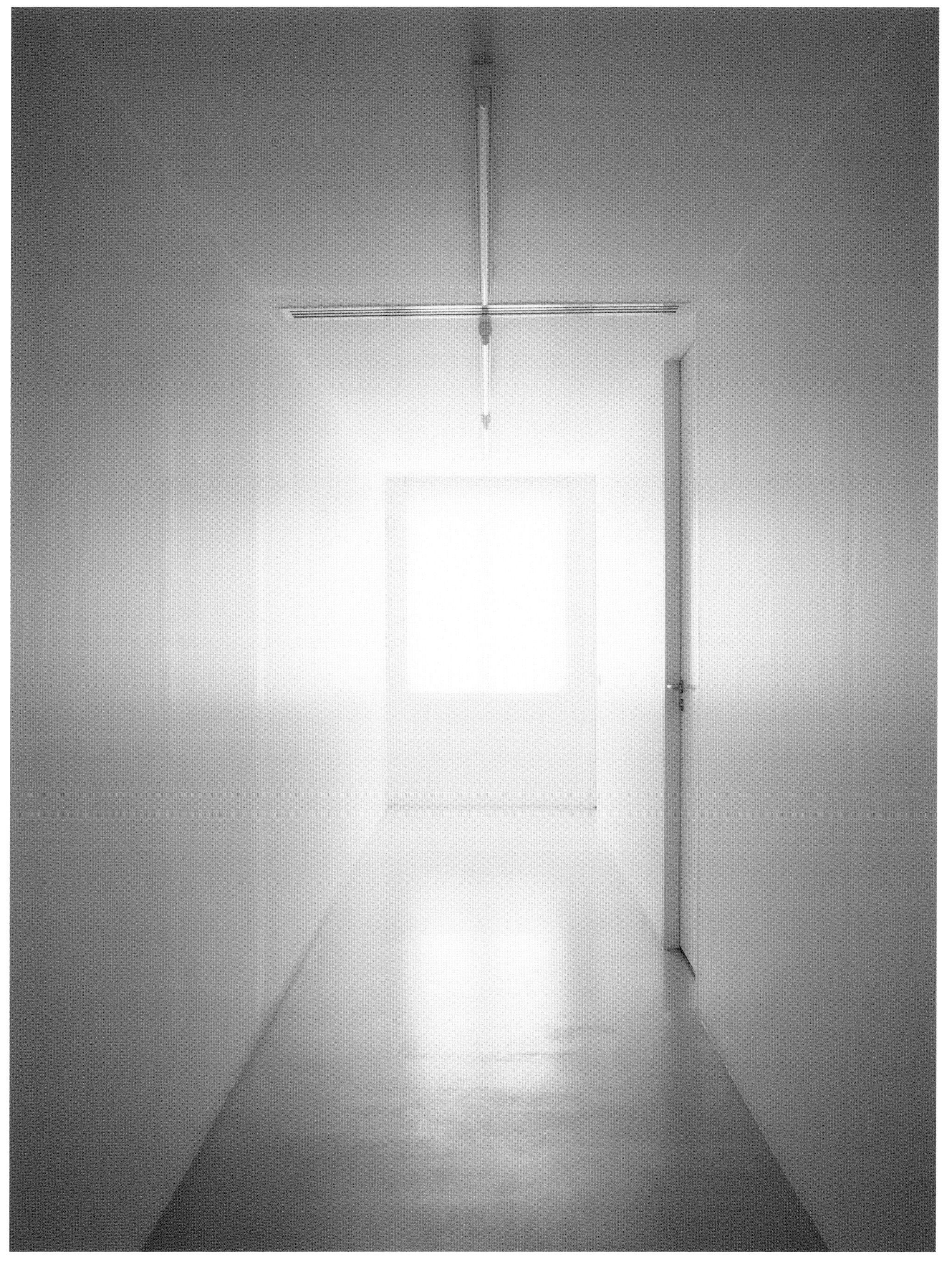

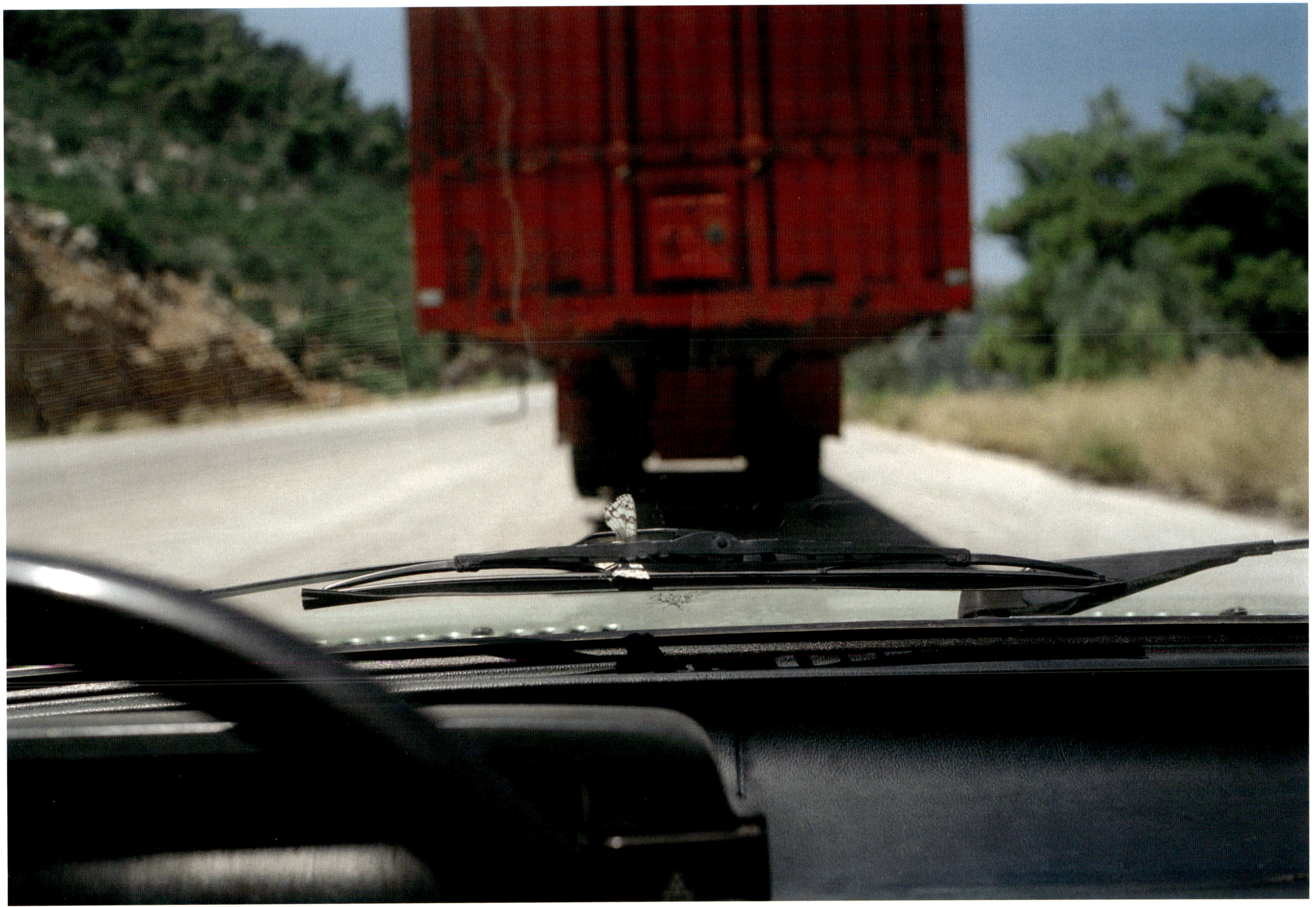

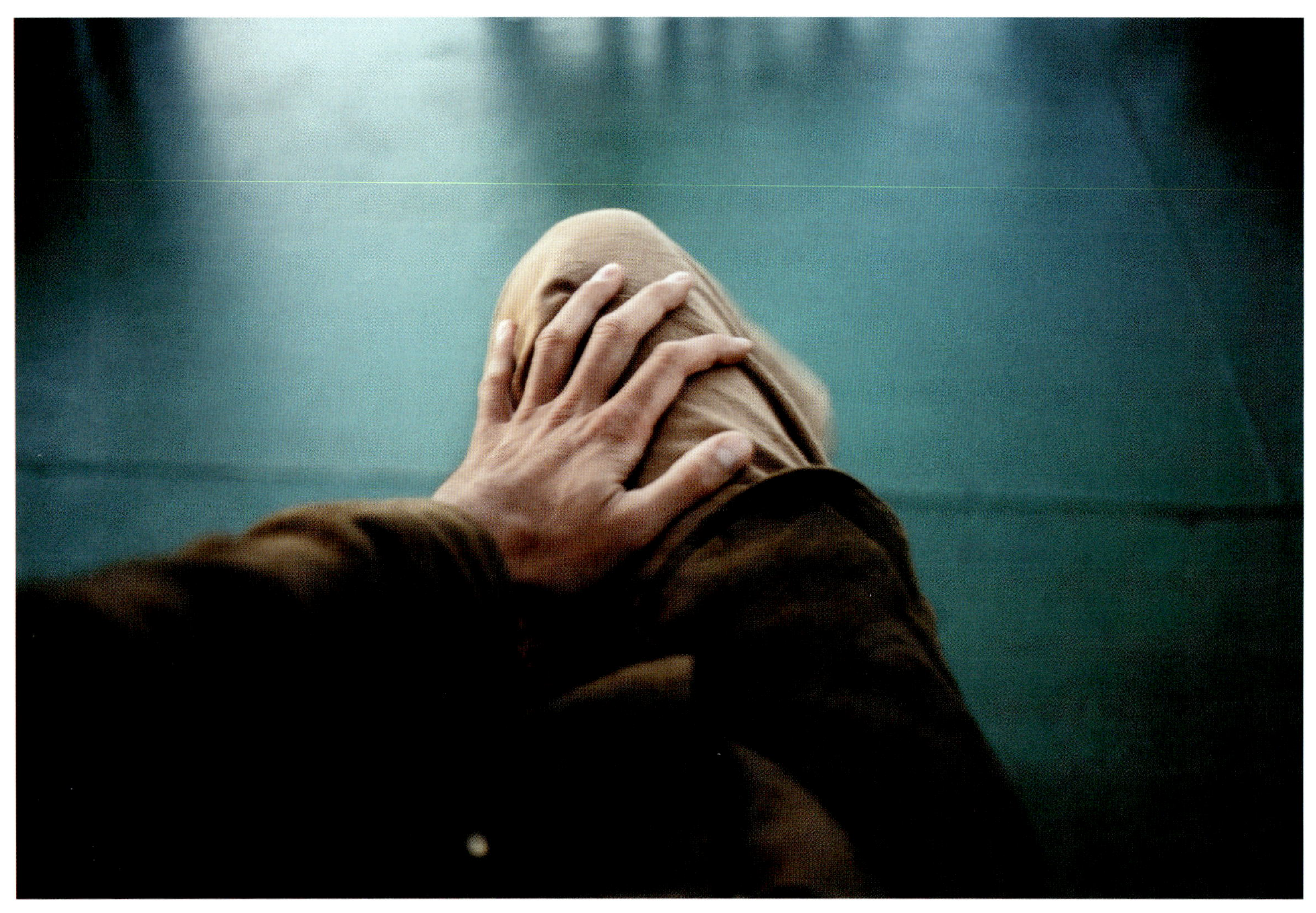

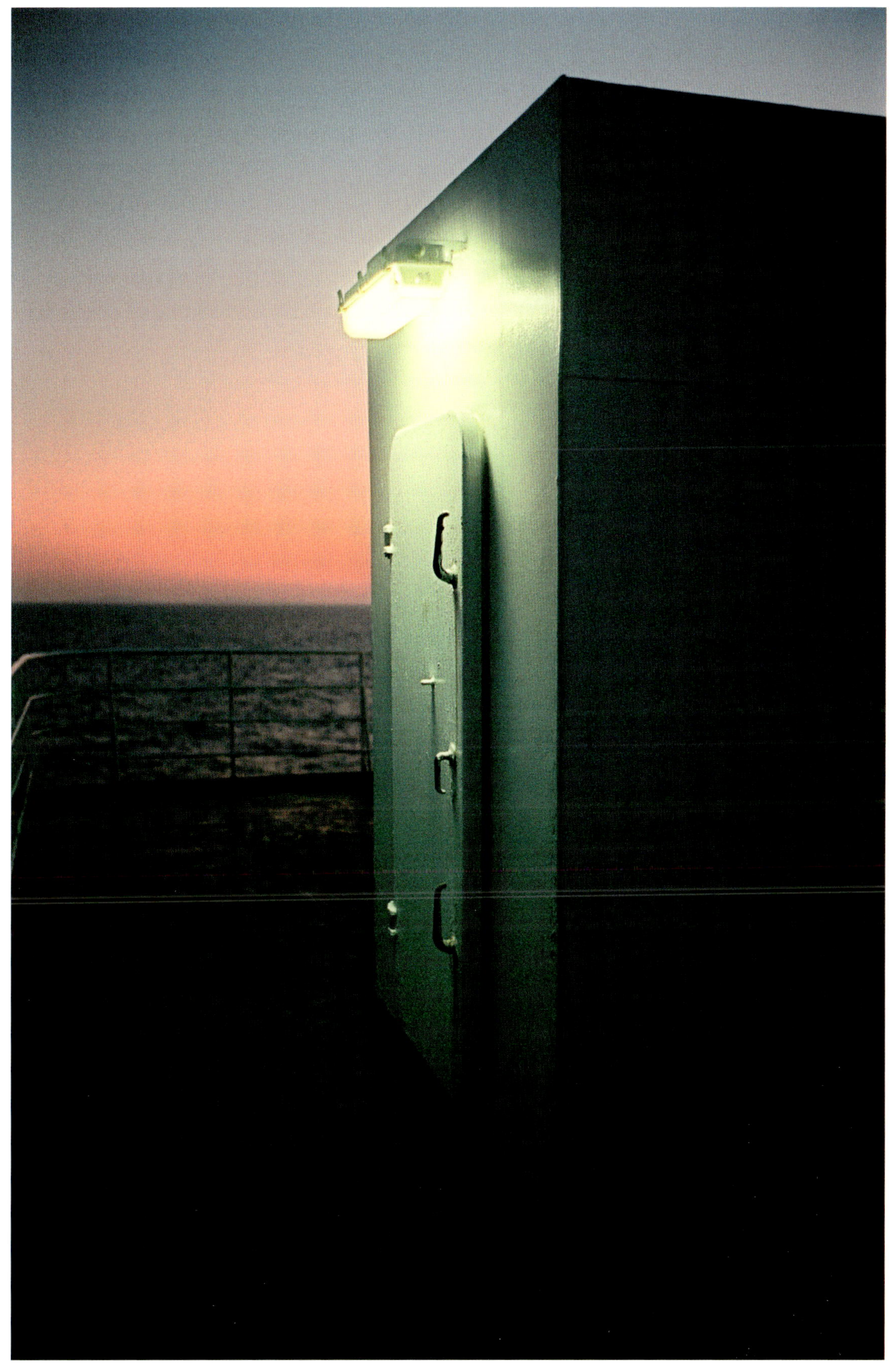

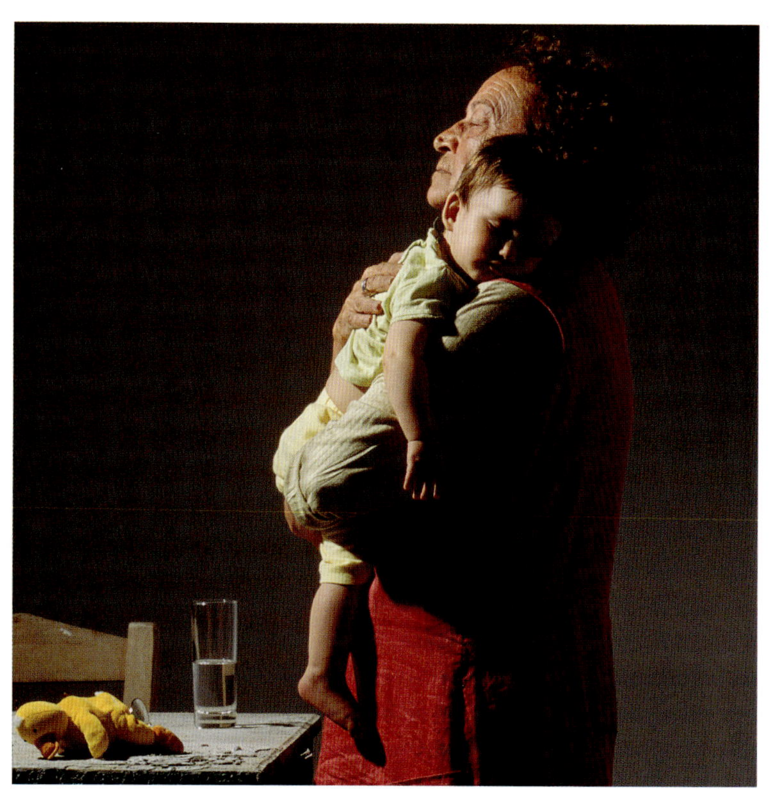

82 / Theoni (detail)

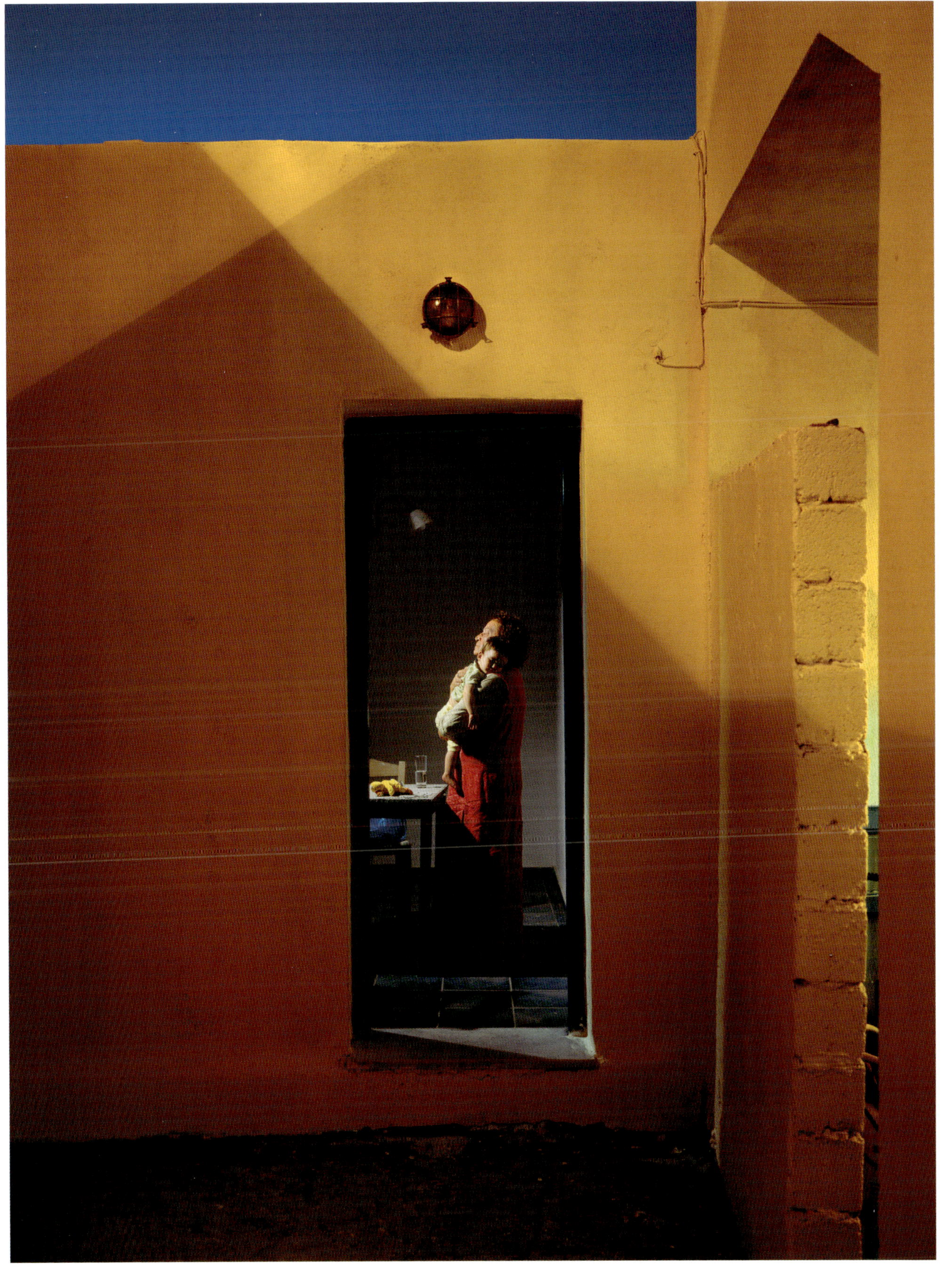

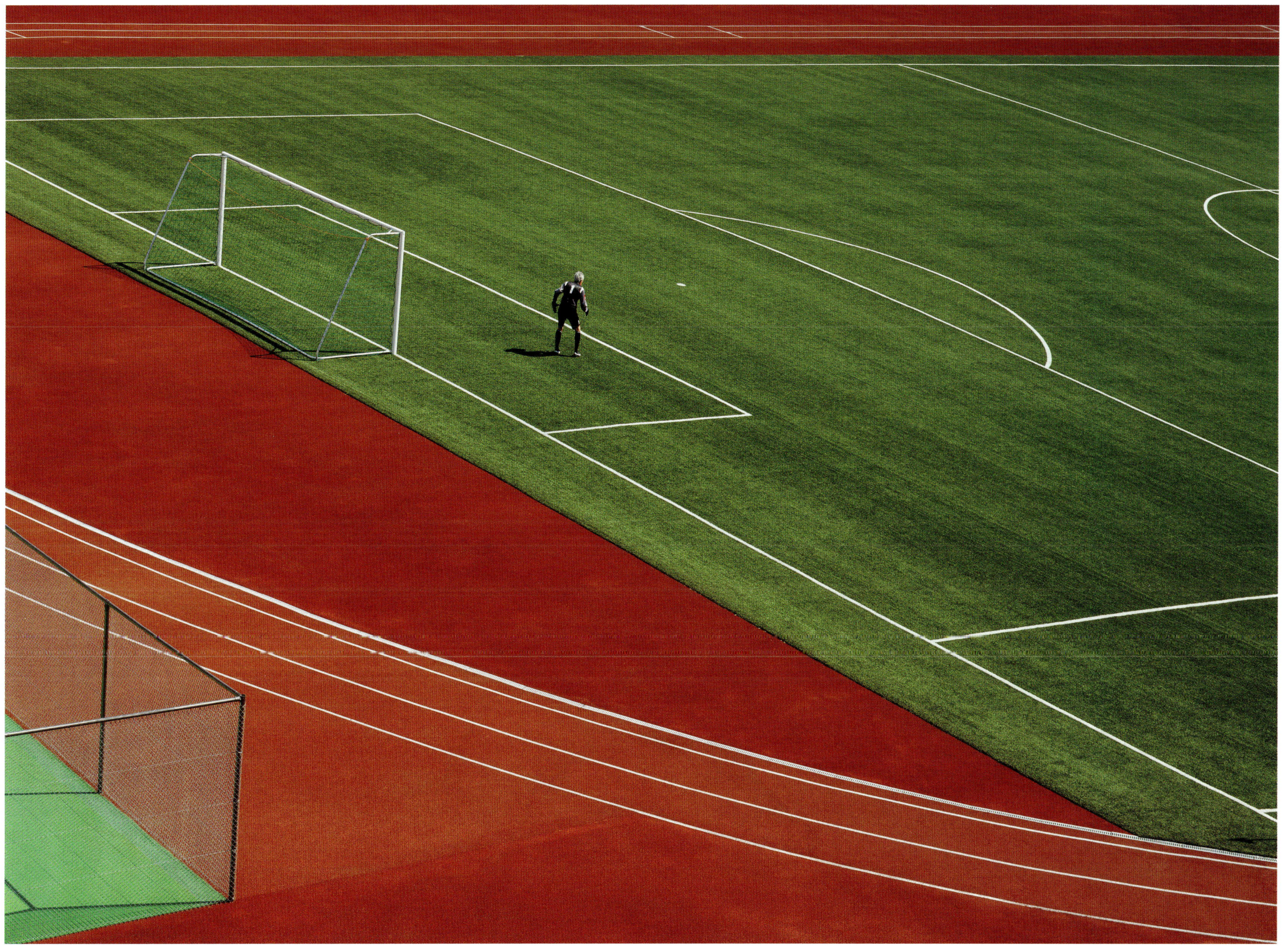

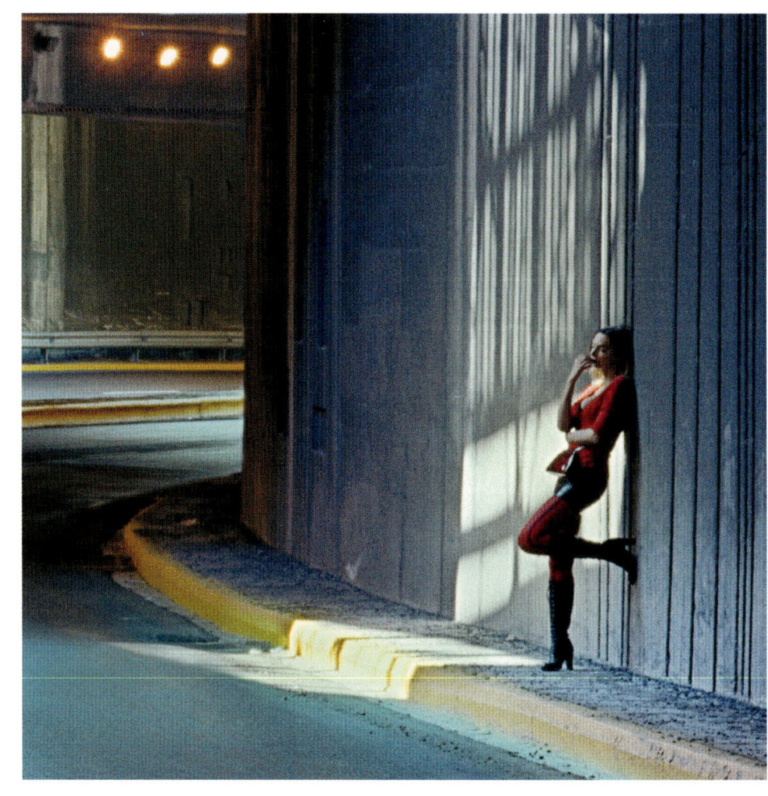

86 / Aliki (detail)

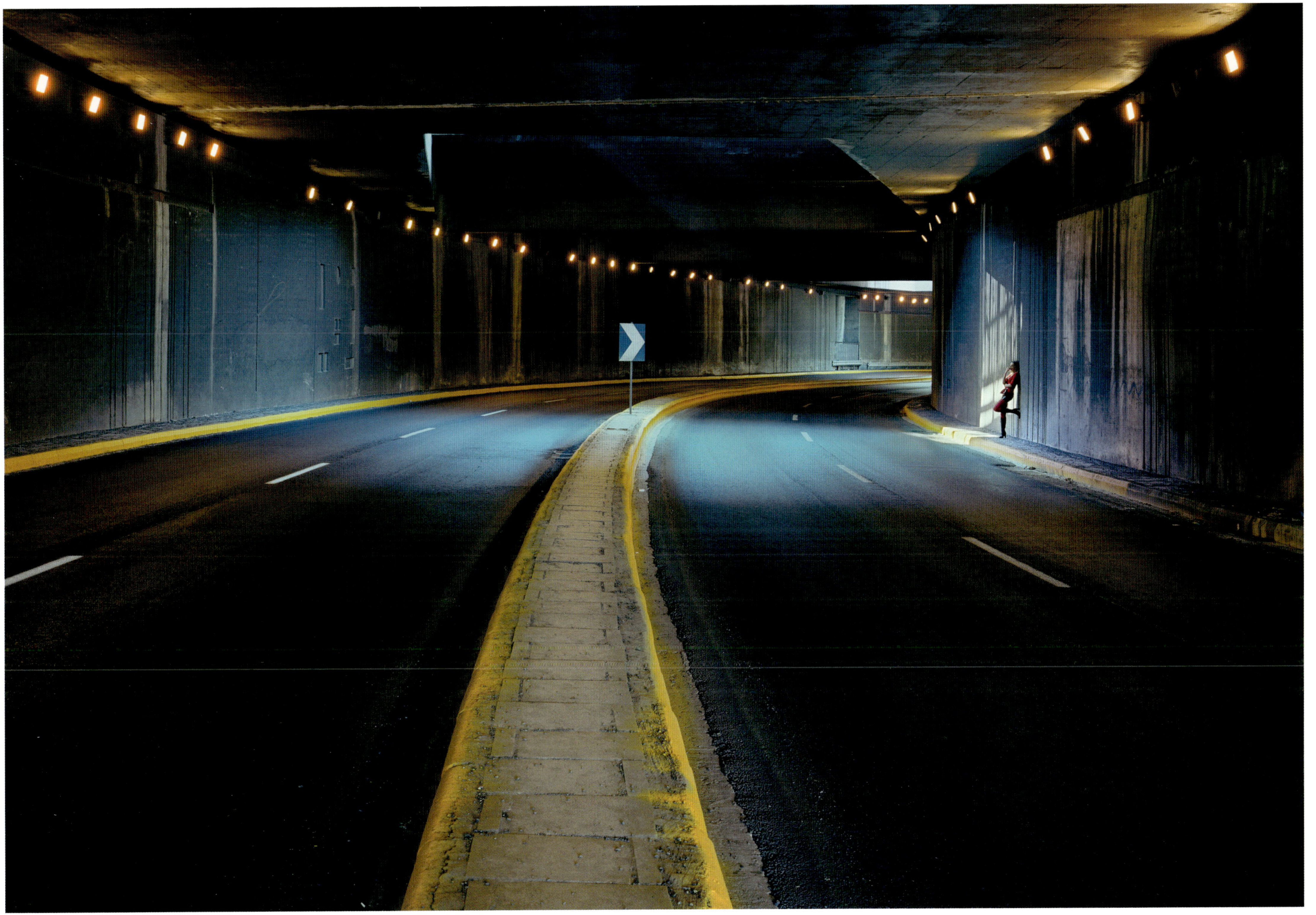

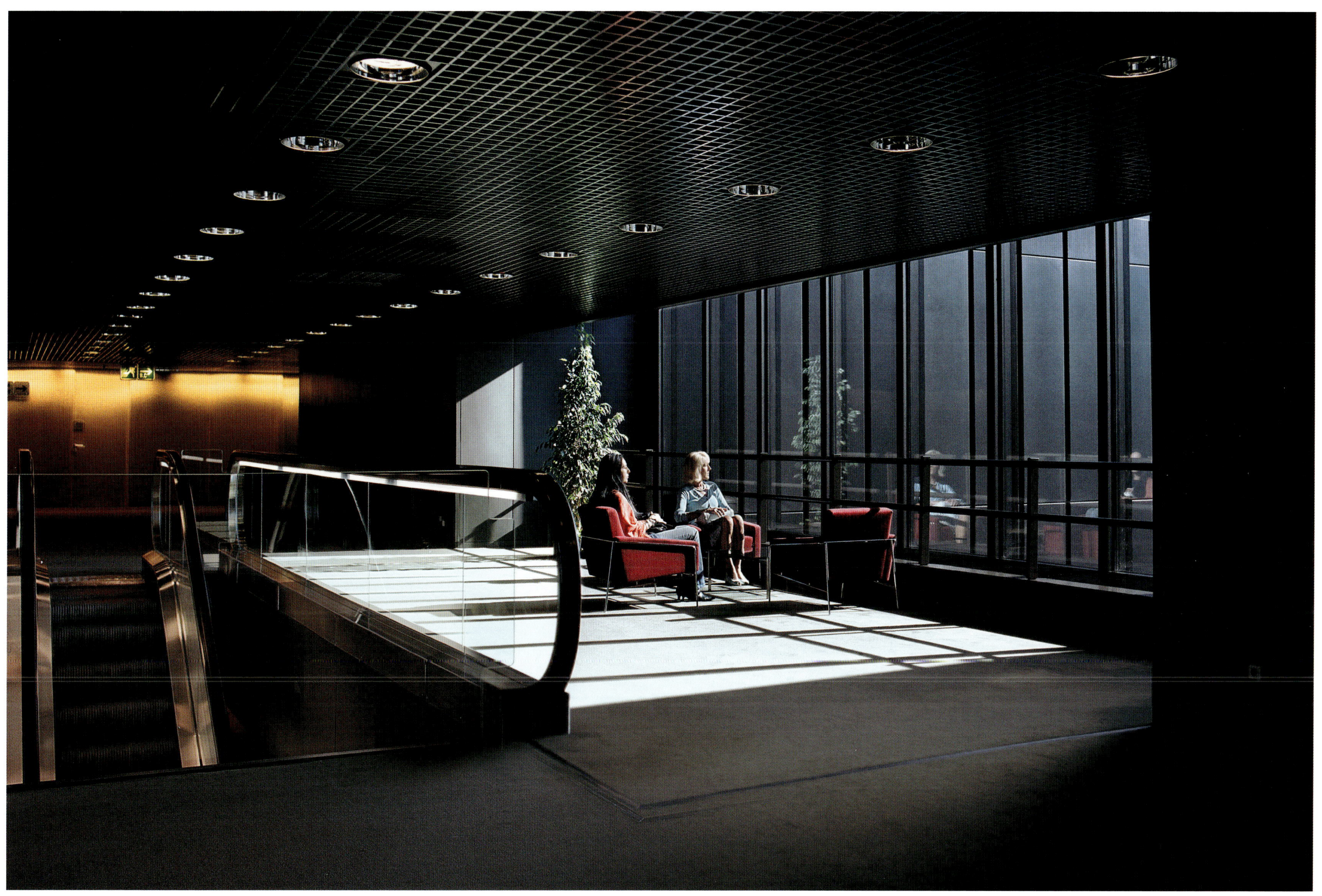

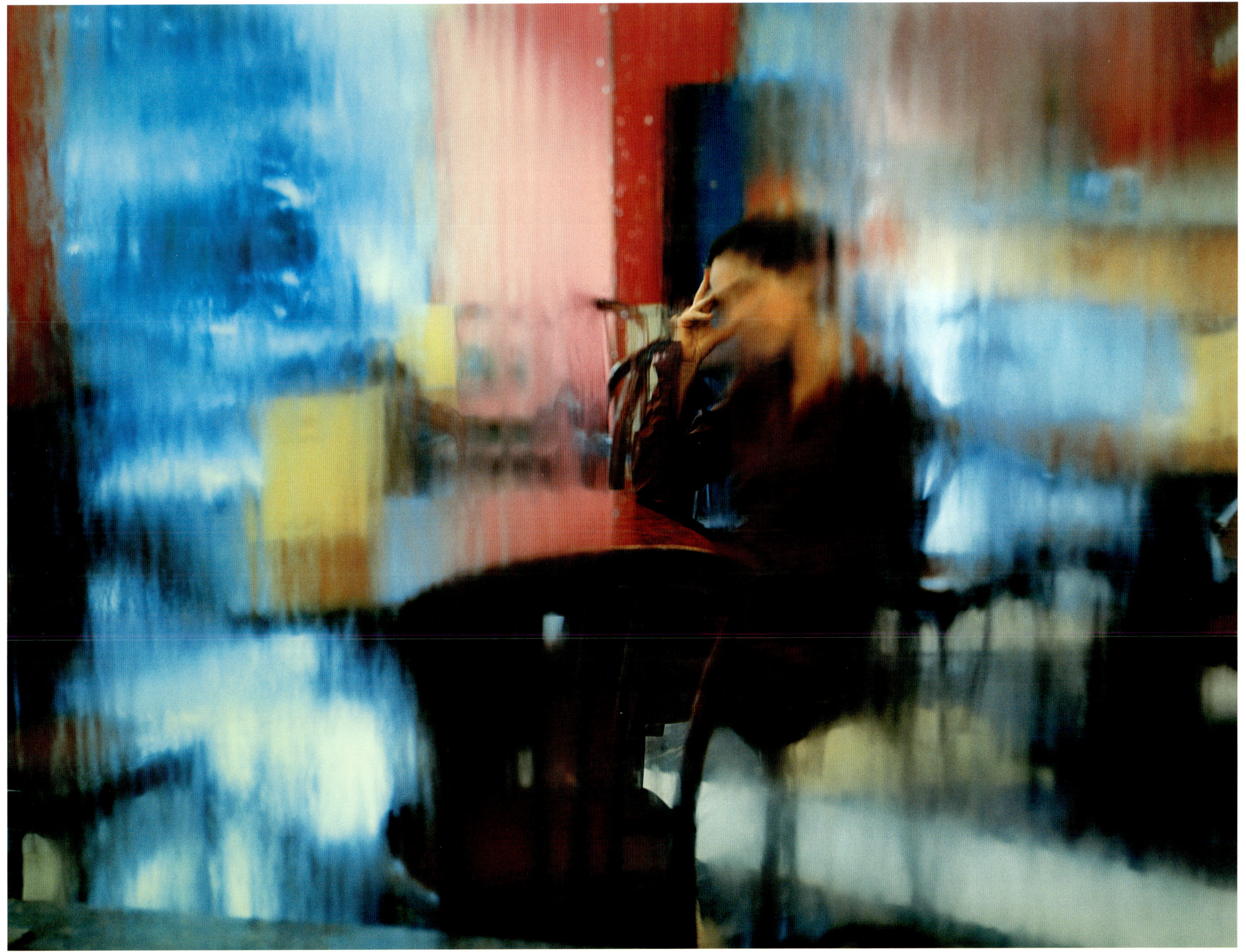

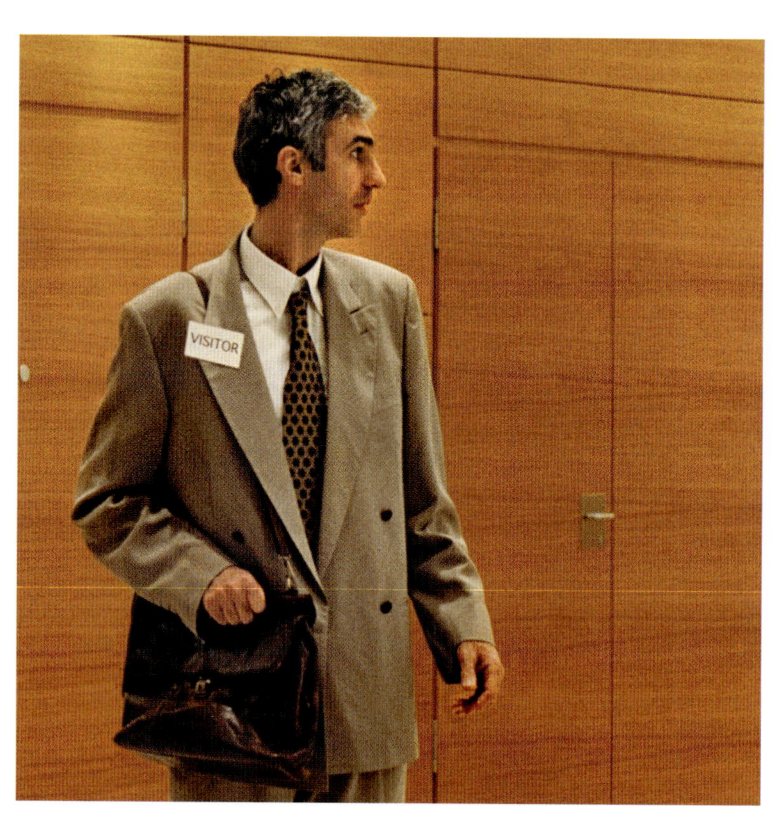

92 / Leonidas (detail)

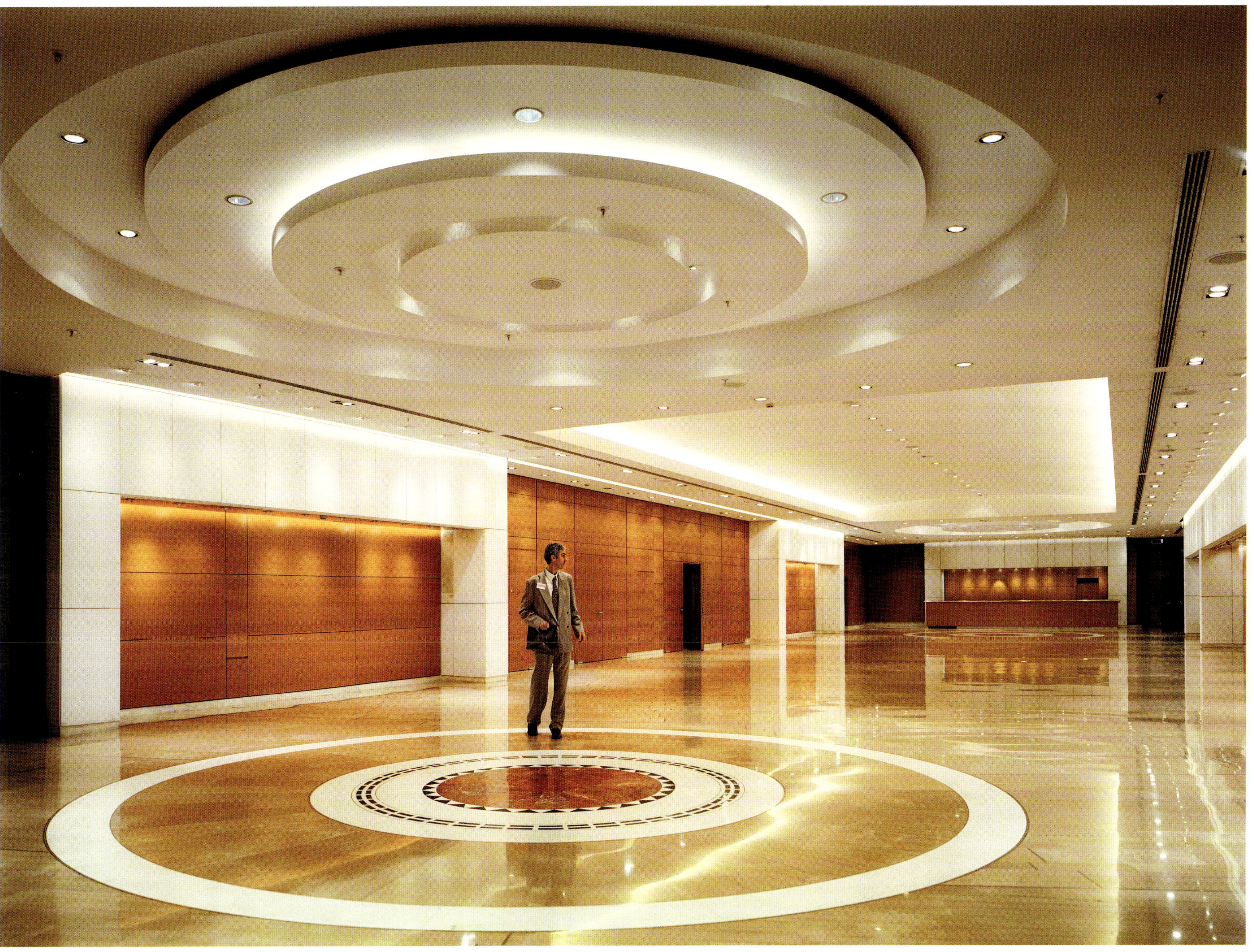

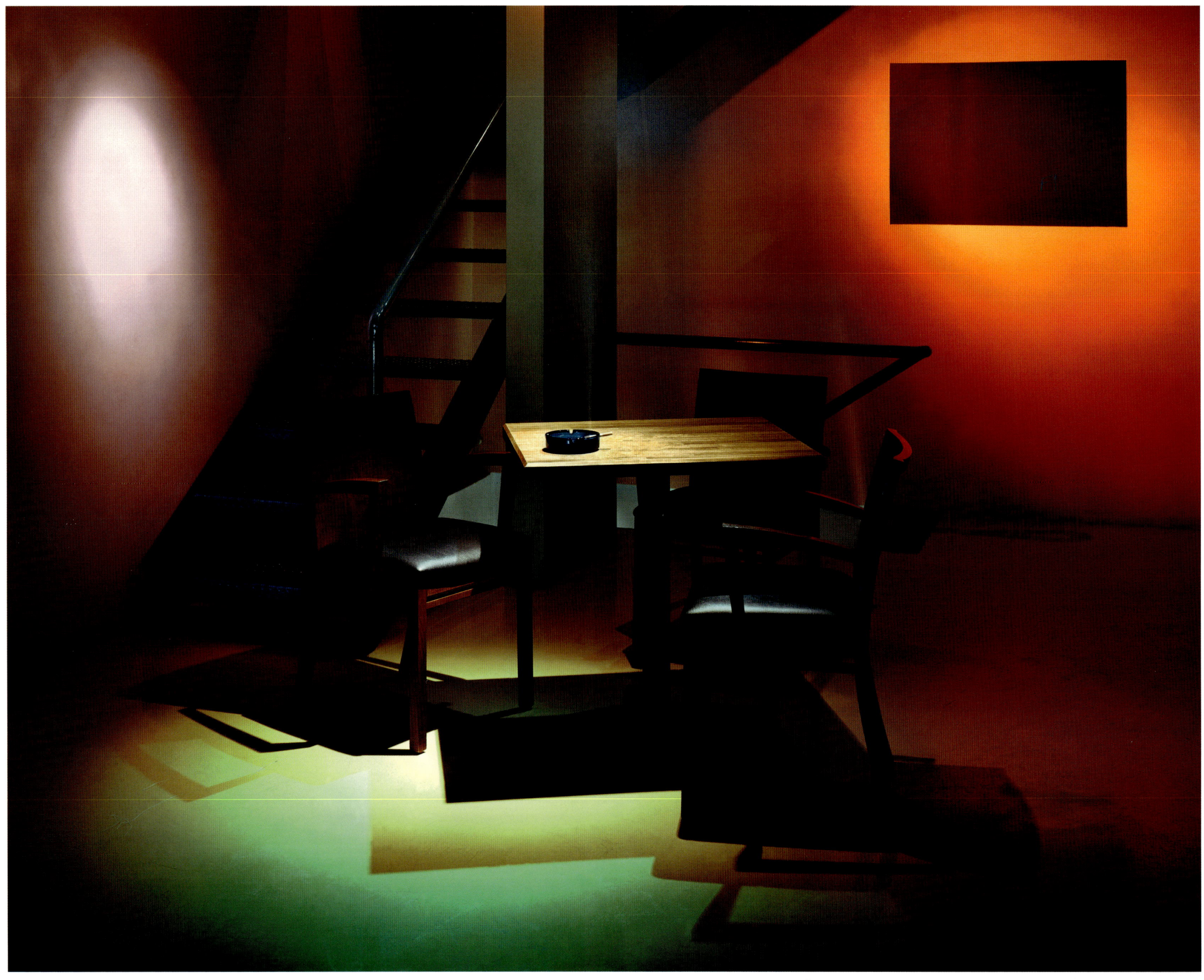

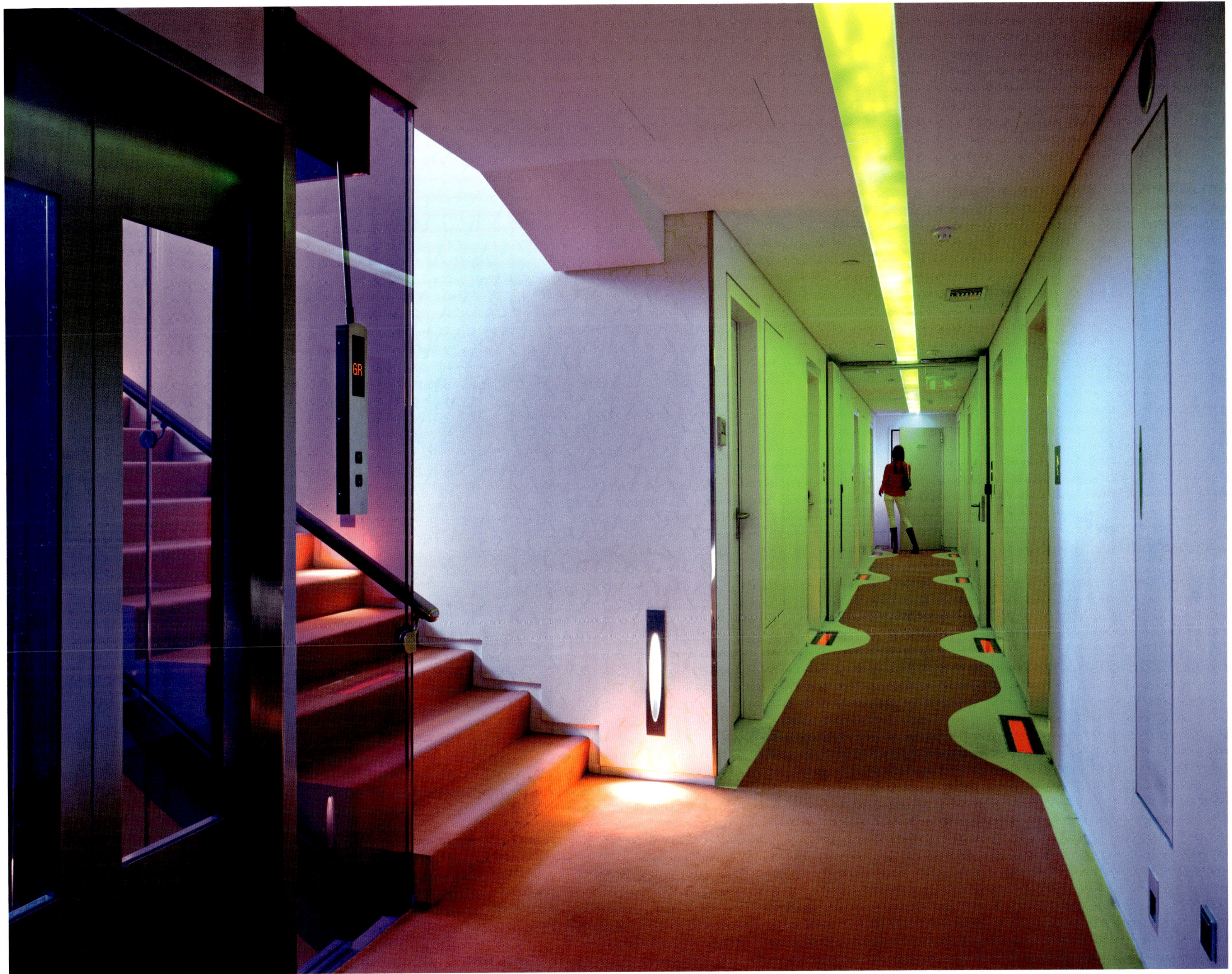

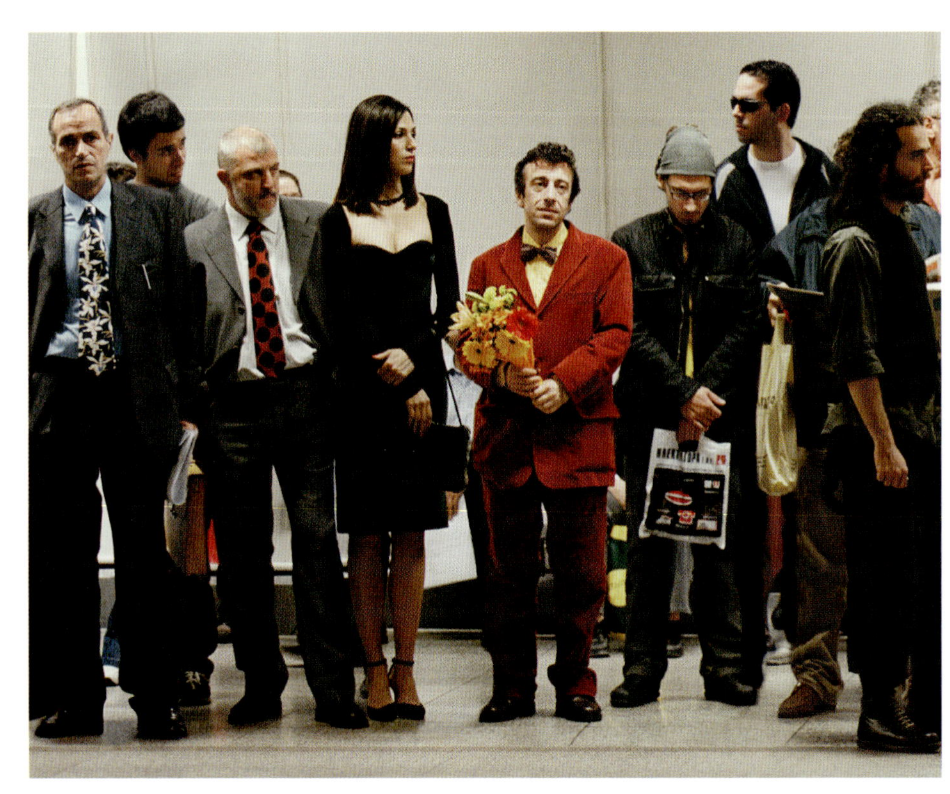

96 / Metro (detail)

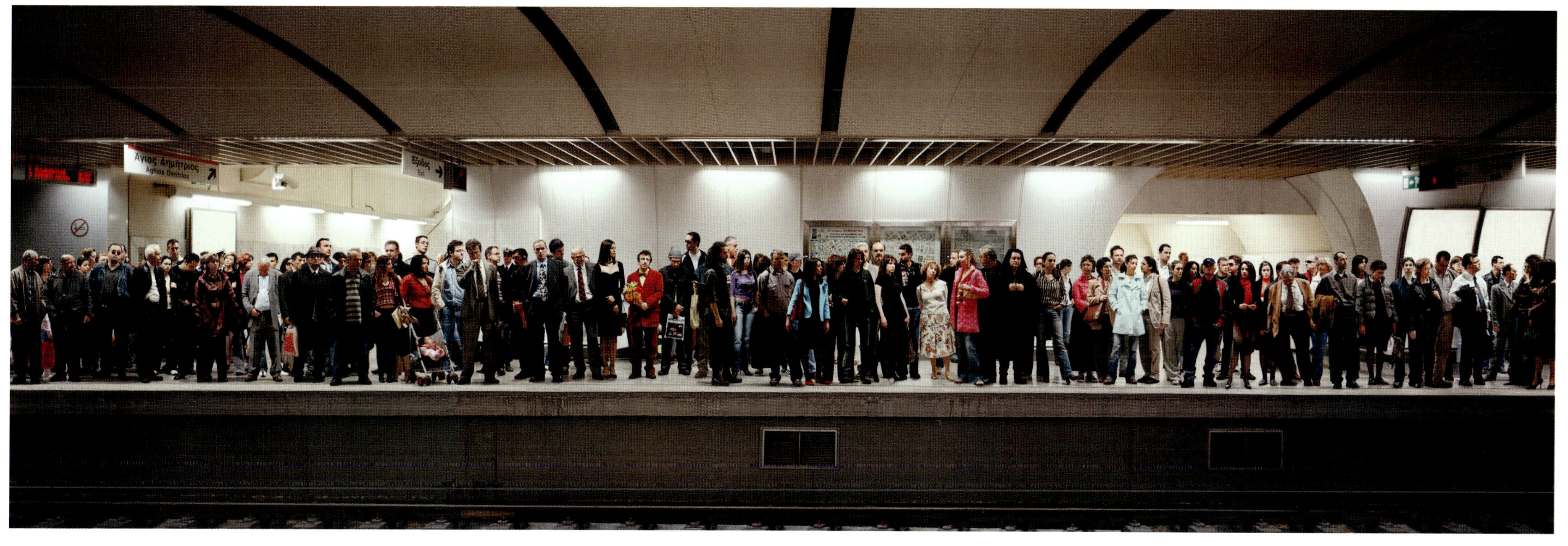

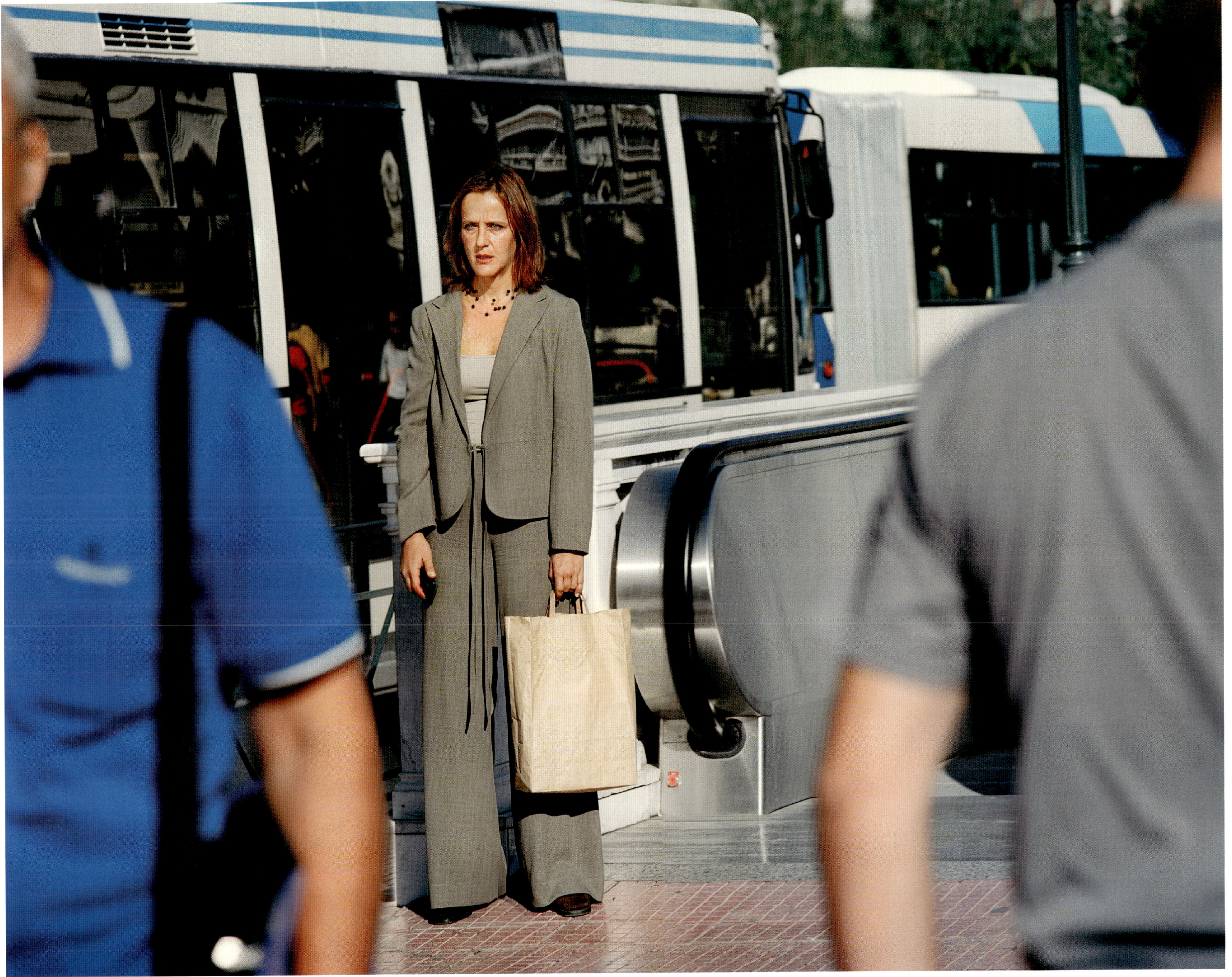

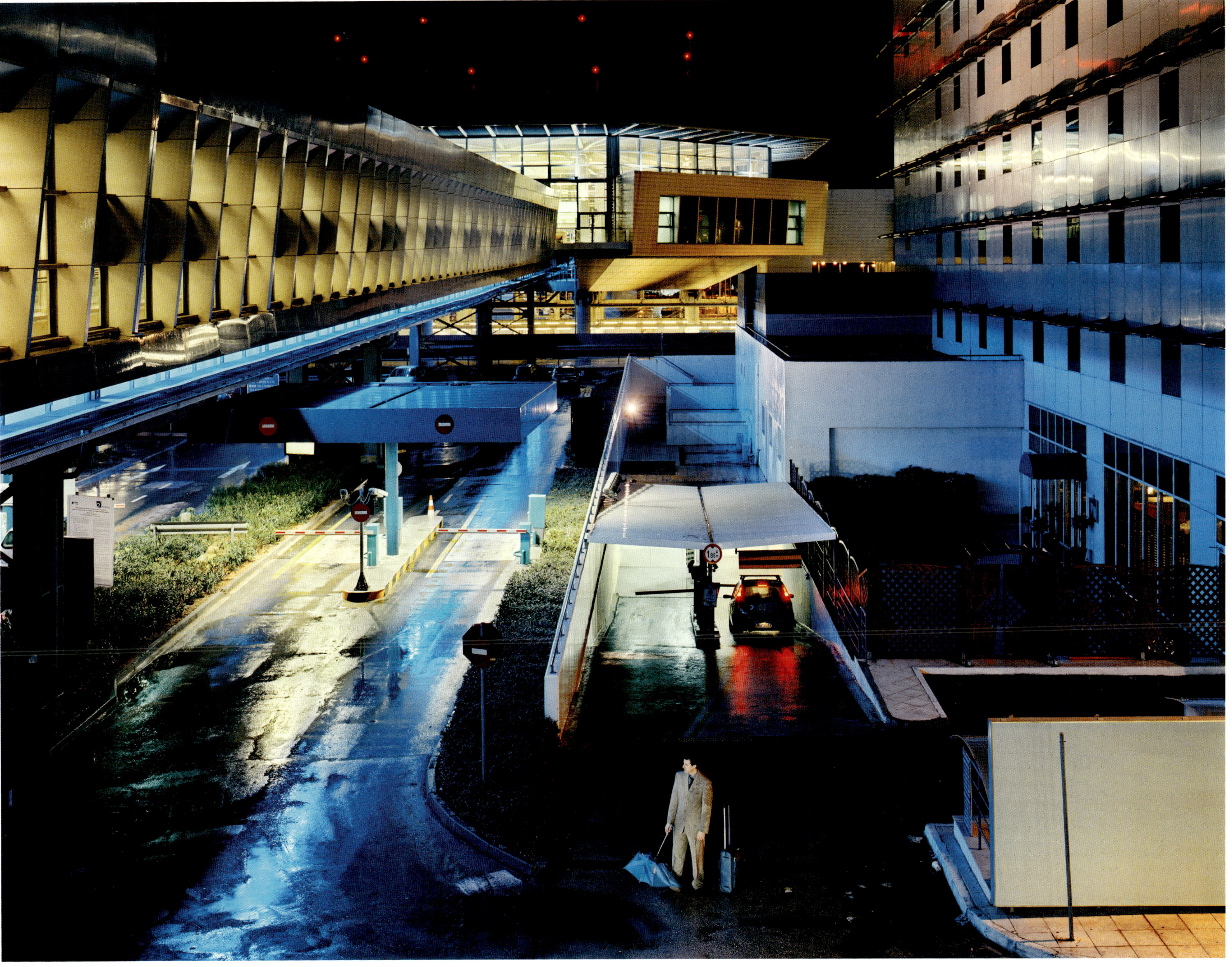

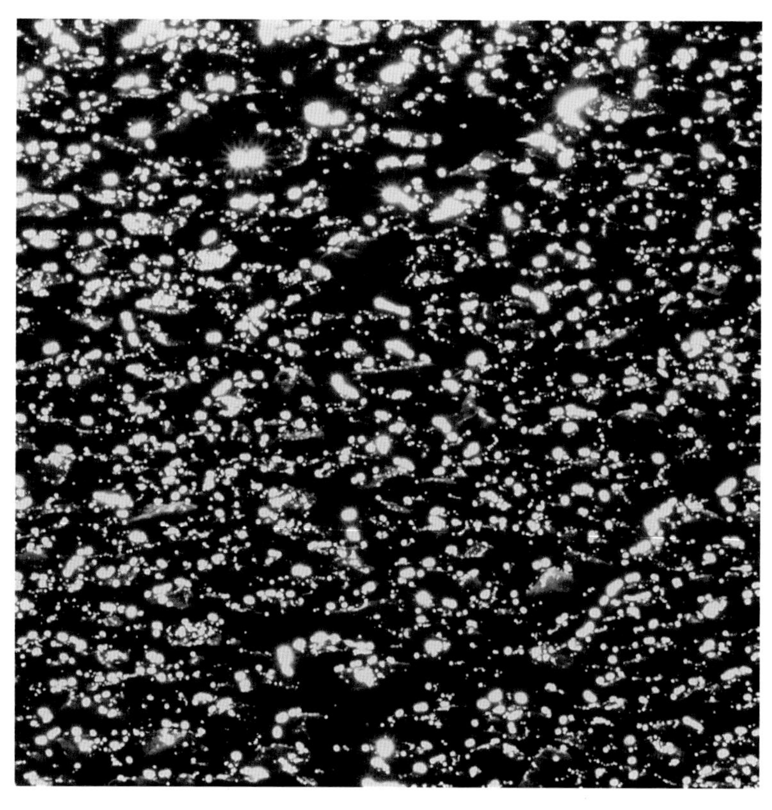

102 / Rain (detail)

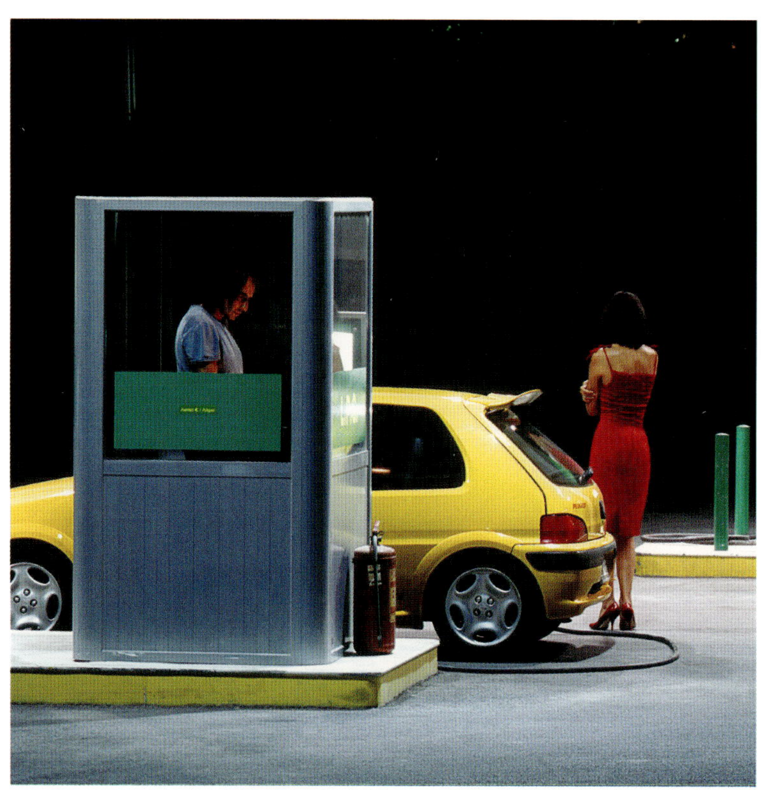

104 / Gas Station (detail)

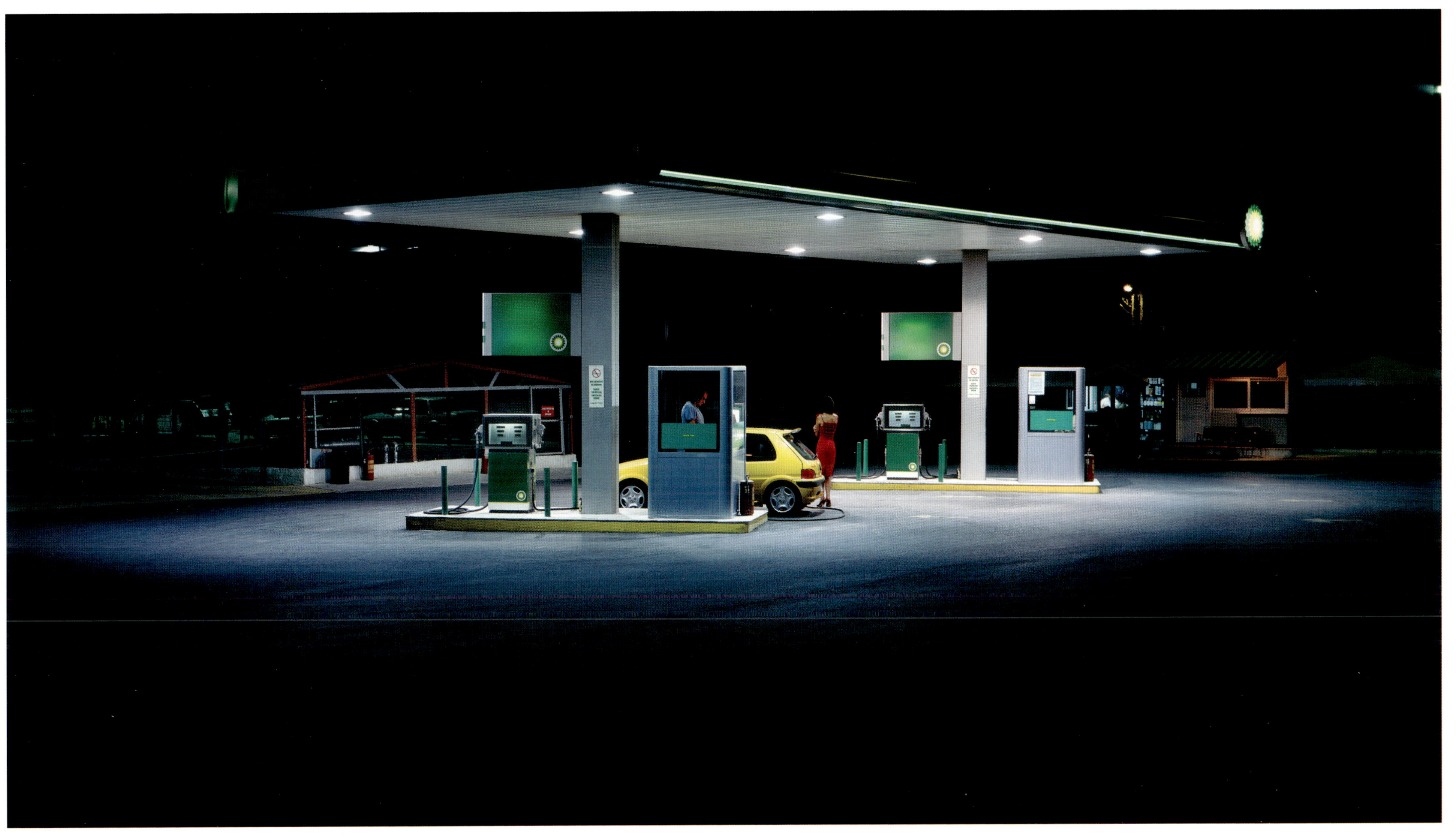

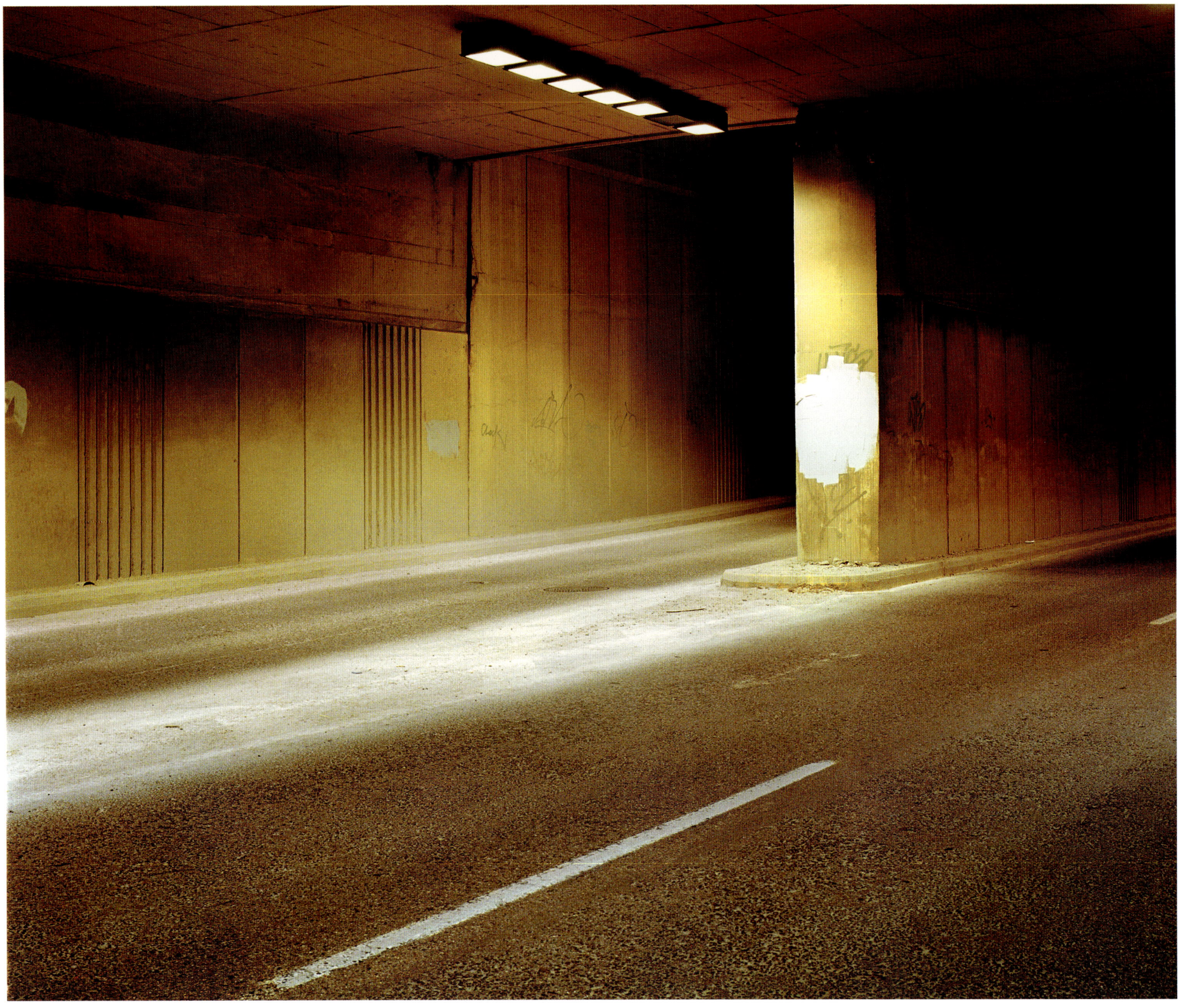

106 / Underpass

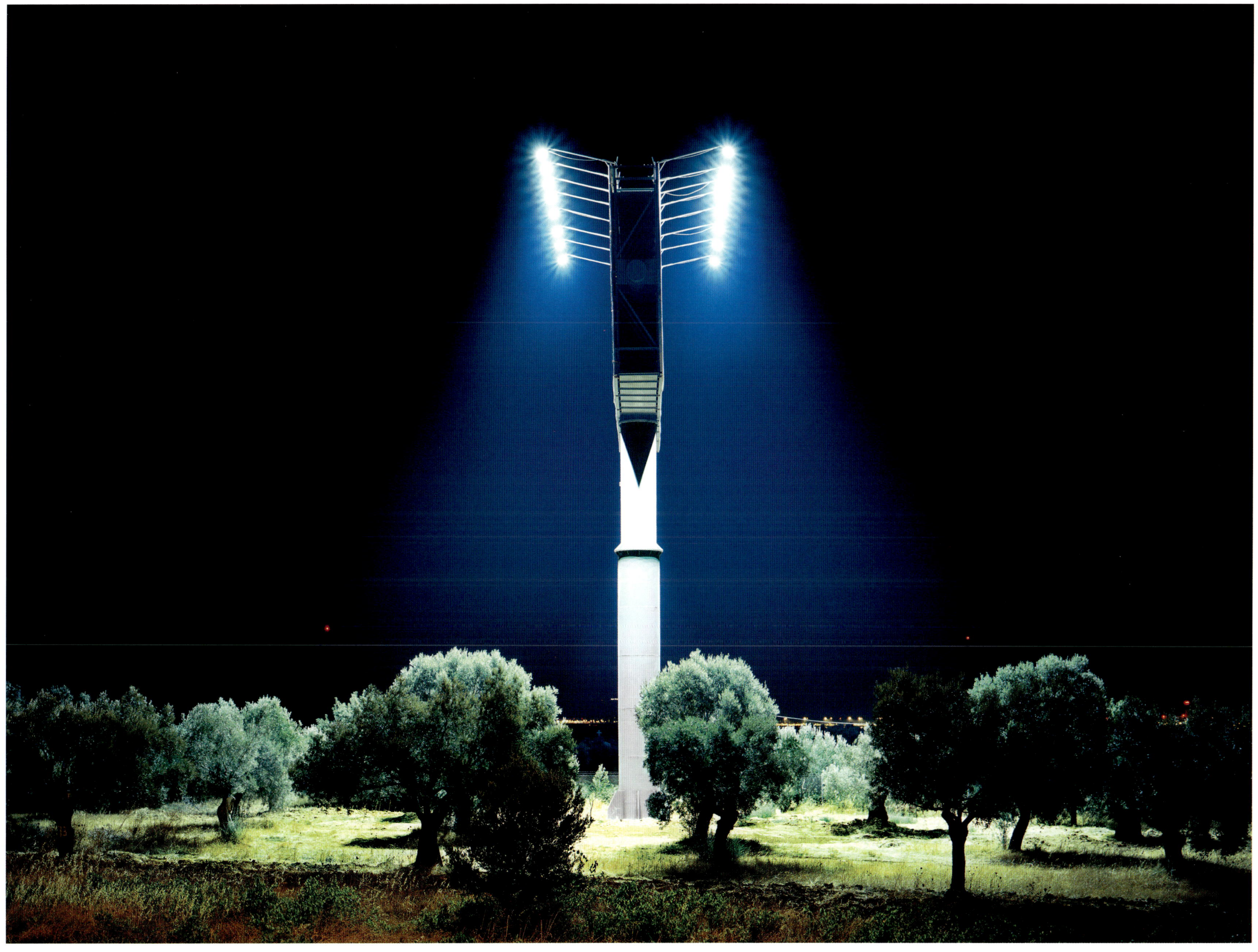

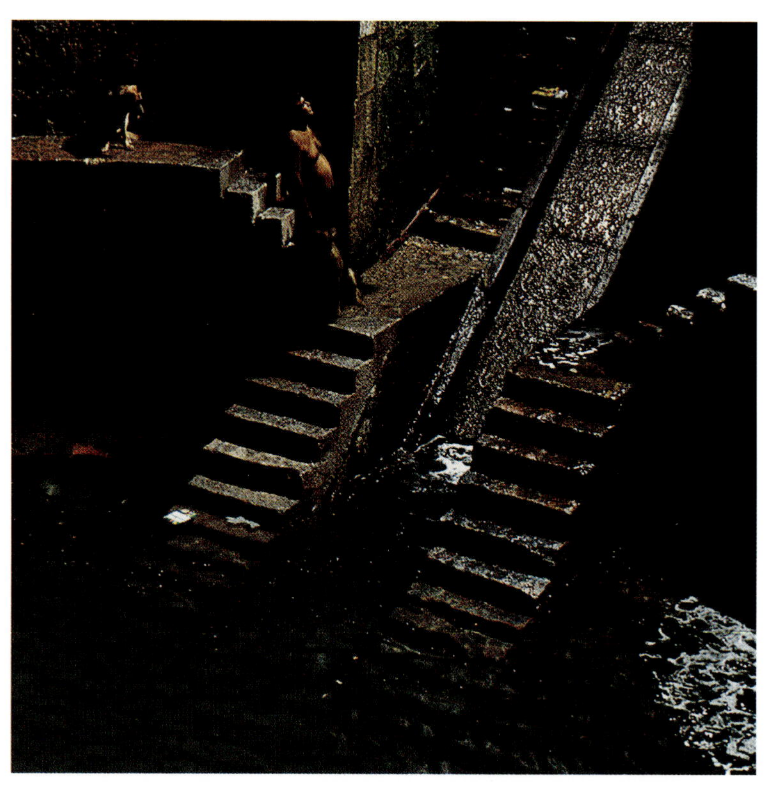

108 / Piraeus (detail)

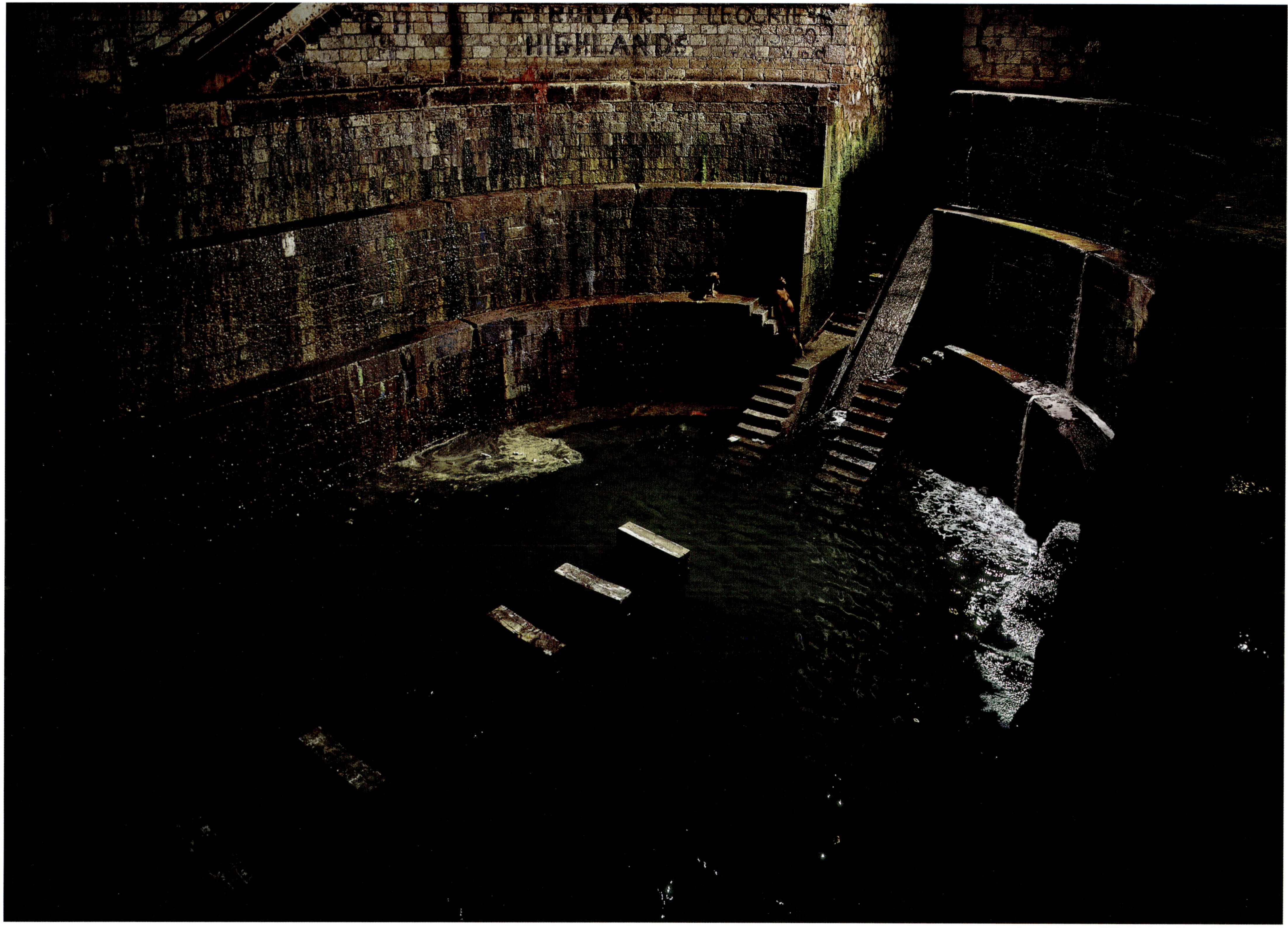

HIGHLANDS

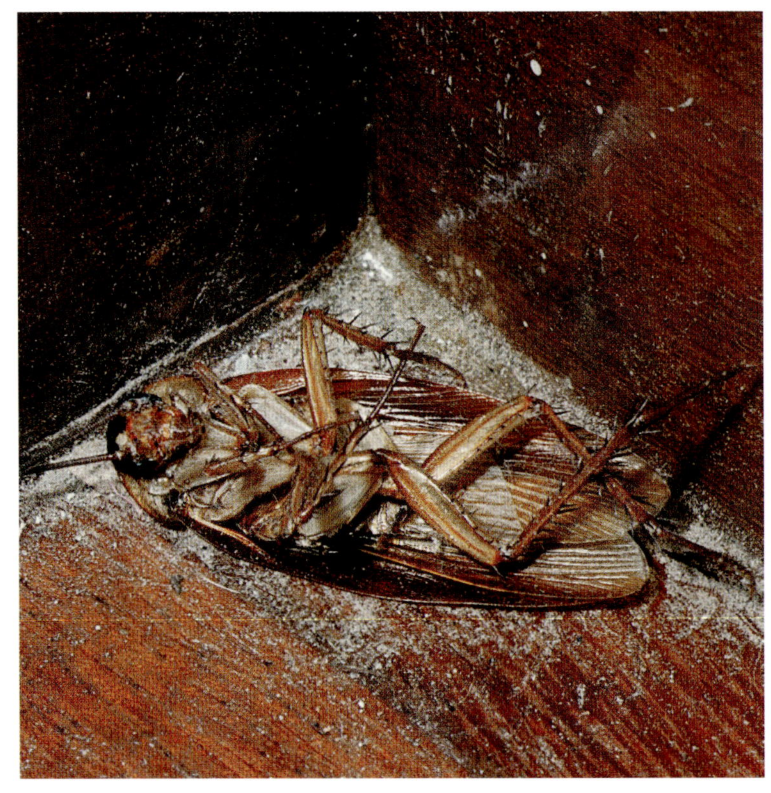

110 / Cockroach (detail)

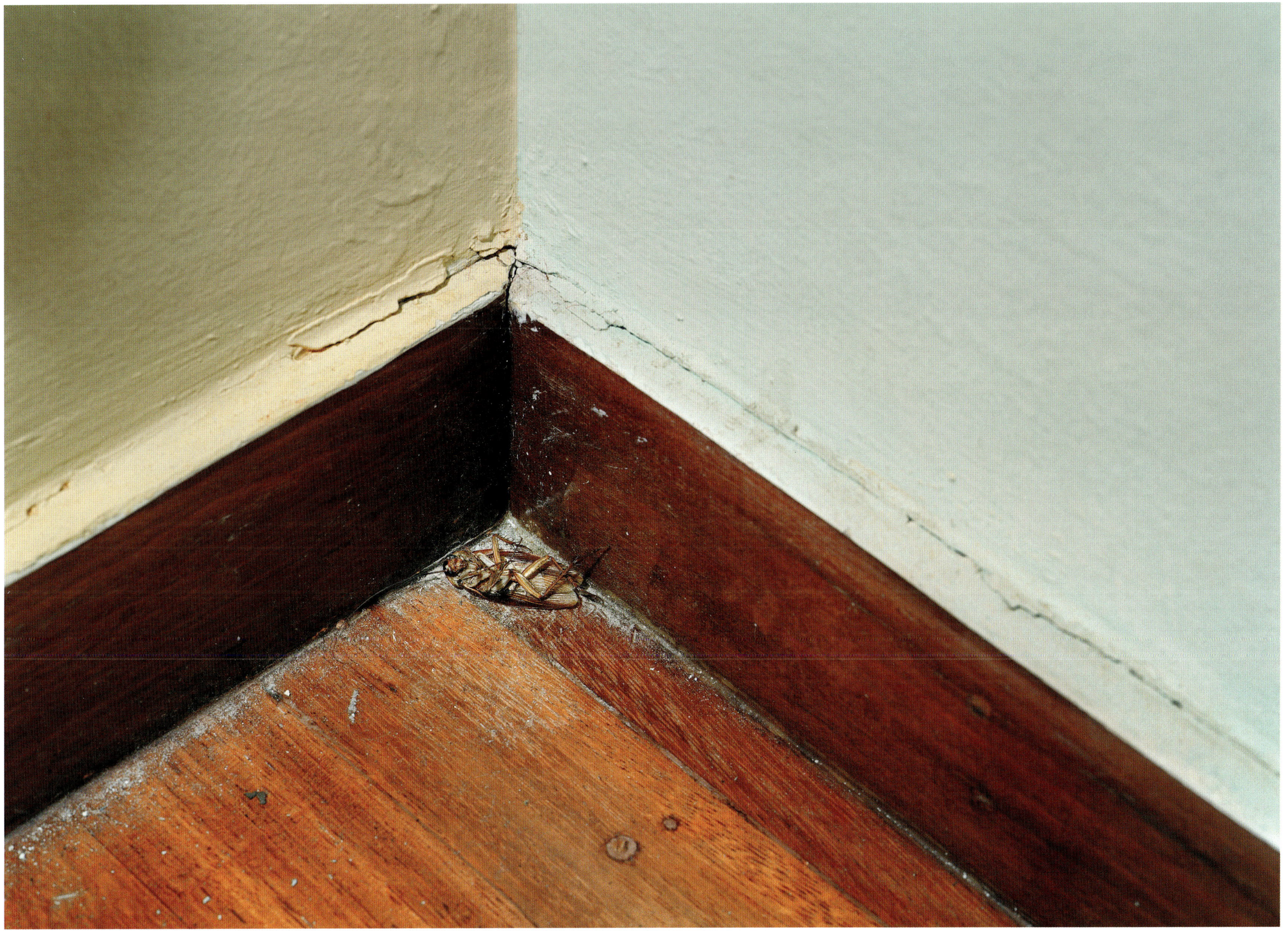

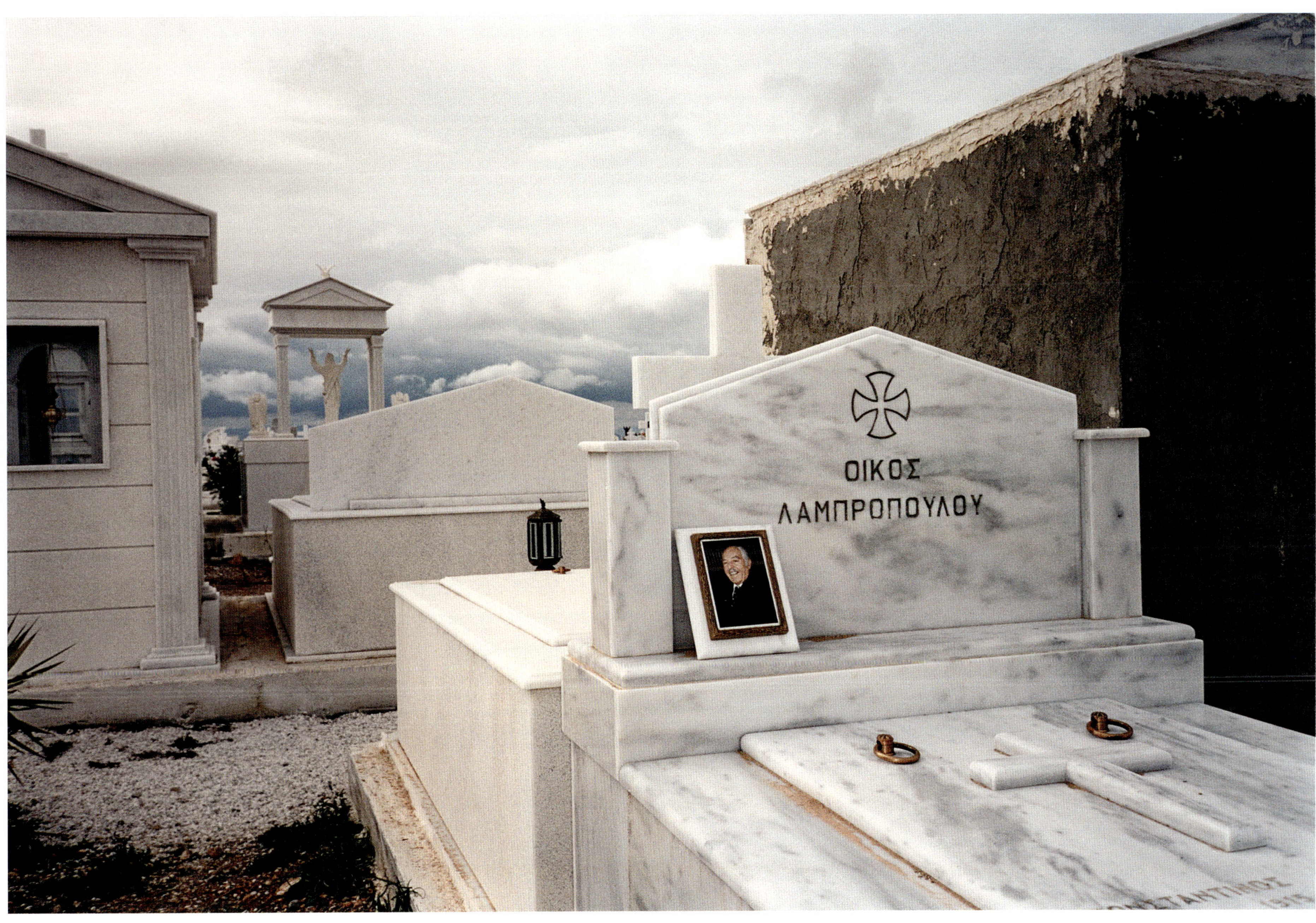

ΟΙΚΟΣ
ΛΑΜΠΡΟΠΟΥΛΟΥ

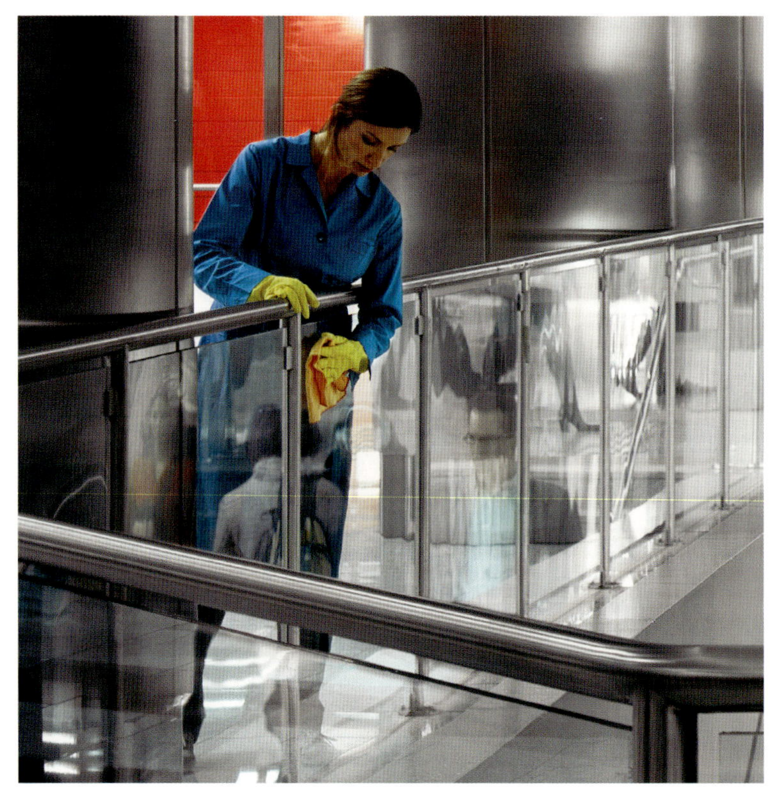

114 / Urania (detail)

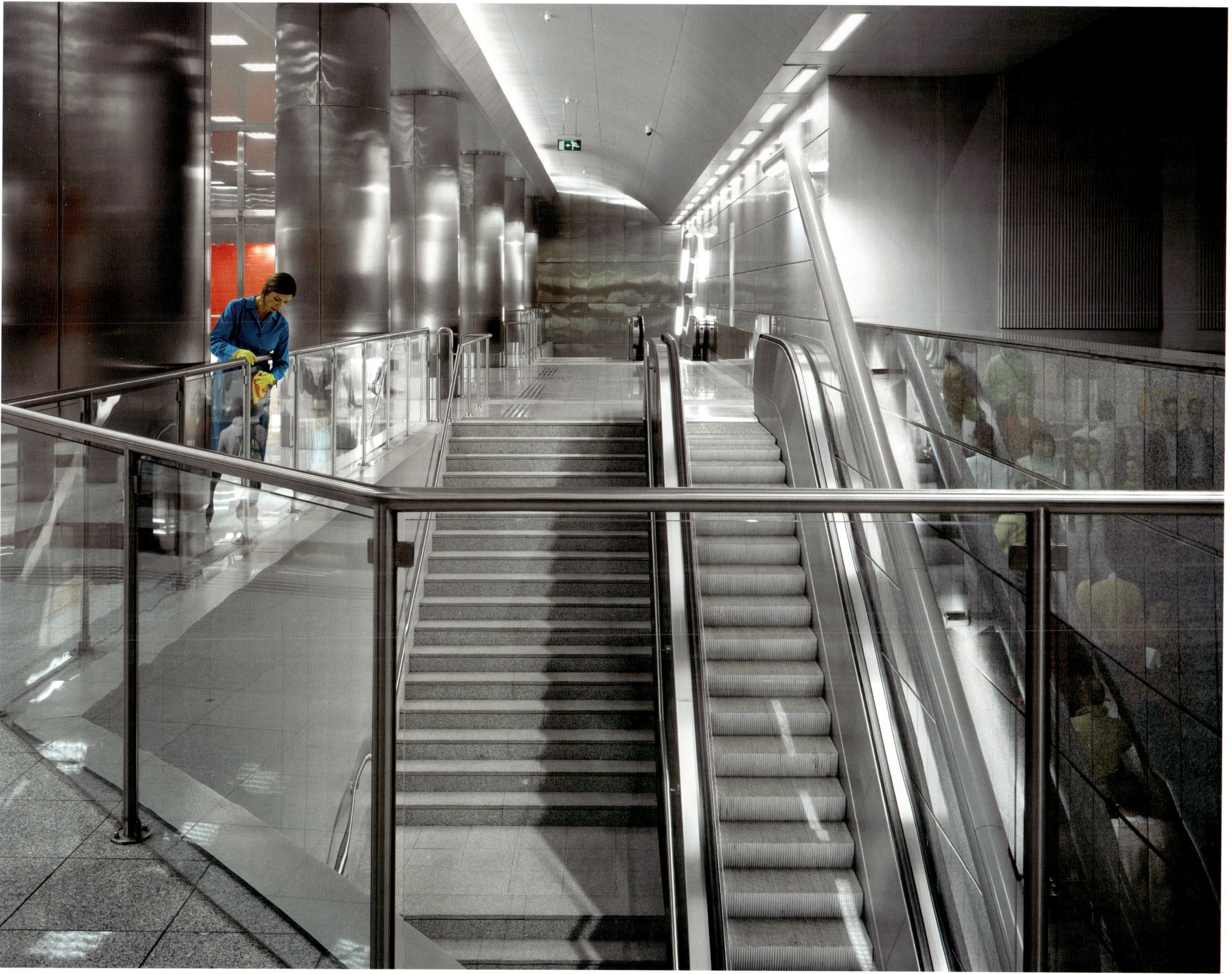

The Determinate and Indeterminate Gaze
in the Photographs of Panos Kokkinias

Régis Durand

The photographs of Panos Kokkinias show scenes or situations that are generally impossible to define, and this indeterminacy extends even to the beholder's response. Yes, we could attempt to find (or project) a narrative element, to pick out the traces of an "incident," of something that might have happened or be about to happen, but the distance is so great, the human figure (if there is one) so tiny and lost in the immensity of its setting, that it is difficult to muster sufficient narrative energy to breathe life into a story or scene. Or, if we do try, the effort is detached, as if we were simply exercising our interpretative faculties. Whatever we do, in any case, the space that we enter is indecisive and hypothetical.

For one thing, everything in these photos has manifestly been calculated, right down to the smallest details, apparently leaving no room for what Lee Friedlander calls the "generosity" of photography—"the fact," as Michael Fried writes, "that photographs typically depict a wealth of detail that the photographer taking the picture never quite perceived as such, much less intended to photograph."[1] If there is a possibility of different interpretations, this is not because we have discovered something that the photographer did not notice, a kind of gift, but rather because of the strict framework he has put in place. In this sense, Kokkinias is an exponent of the "theatricality" described (and, since 1967, doggedly opposed) by Fried, a form of indeterminacy which postulates that the meaning of the work is the one given to it by each beholder.

But, on the other hand, as I have suggested, this possibility seems at the same time to be denied us, precisely because the composition is so precise and constrained. Everything points to the conclusion that we are bound to read these photographs as the artist who made them meant them to be read, yet we have no way of knowing what that is. This apparent contradiction is, I think, what gives Kokkinias' photos their charm, and how he very consciously locates his work outside the perimeter of a number of major practitioners who might come to mind (but more on them later).

A first observation one can make is that time seems suspended here—and not only as it is, by definition, in any photograph. It is suspended in several ways: by the fact, for example,

that nothing is really happening on the stage of the representation. Everything has already happened (which is classically photographic) or about to happen (which evokes other practices: narrative in general, and a certain kind of painting).

But this suspension of time also involves a particular visual treatment, the absorption of the small cell of the event or narrative into a vast "landscape," as if it were frozen in the relative scale of vision. This frozen quality to some extent recalls the mood that permeates the paintings of Hopper, which are bathed in a distinctive light and immobility suggestive of what one might call an empty waiting: waiting without an object. This was already the case in Kokkinias' first photographs, where the contrast of scale between the frame and the figure or "event" is not so marked. The effect in these pieces is due, rather, to the incongruous presence of objects such as the chicken in a freezer (*Freezer,* p 7), or the plate of spaghetti on a table (*Spaghetti,* p 11). But, in that second photo, as indeed in *Meat* (p 9), there is already a hint of the implicit presence of a figure and an action. The position of the various elements in the scene, such as the knife, conveys the imminence of action, and implicitly suggests the presence, albeit enigmatic, of a human character in the sequence constituted by *Peanuts* (p 10), *Cabinet* (p 13), and *Laughter* (p 17).

With *Interiors* (pp 19–37) we again find the enigma of an empty space, with only clues to a hypothetical presence (a mattress, a lit chandelier, a door ajar), as opposed to the solitary figure dwarfed by its surroundings in works such as *Swimming Pool* (p 31) and *Crawling* (p 37).

Henceforth, the apparatus is in place for a meditation on a contemporary form of visuality, reactivating and revisiting a number of questions from the history of painting. First of all, naturally, there is the figure/ground relation, which is a major theme in recent series such as *Here We Are* (pp 73–115) and *Landscapes* (pp 39–71).

The figure (or the trace of their presence) is barely discernible in the immensity of a landscape that is completely empty and more often than not desolate. The dominant impression here is one of finiteness, a crushing sensation, with echoes of Breughel's

Fall of Icarus and Piranesi's *The Prisons* (in *Piraeus* [p 109], for example). However, these photographic tableaux, too, are deceptive: where we might expect a tragic vision, as in the work of those two great painters, something occurs to avert it, something playful or absurd (in *Kostas* [p 61], *Fanos* [p 65], or *Kokkinovrahos* [p 59]), or the play of color, literally drowning the figure or the "scenic object," which I call the "potential narrative trigger."

This use of color is a constant in Kokkinias' work. Right from the first pieces we can observe a taste for intense hues that saturate the image and its setting, and that in fact become the place and the image, as in *Blue Room* (p 22) and *Squash* (p 23). The artist has two other ways (at least) of making color a major rhetorical operator. One involves the temptation to monochrome, insofar as this characterizes a disquieting, almost carceral space. I am thinking here of *Tom* (p 26), *Hans* (p 27), *Brian* (p 29), *Dog* (p 32), of those long corridors and nondescript spaces, but also of *Syrna* (p 71), of the water in *Kostas* (p 61), and of *Aghida* (p 52), of the rocky ground in *Kokkinovrahos* (p 59), of the earth in *Lambinou* (p 58), and even the pile of litter and earth in *Vardia* (p 53).

The other is the way of using light like a painter or a lighting cameraman. Thus, *Theoni* (p 83) recalls the lighting of certain Flemish paintings, while the name of Hopper comes spontaneously to mind when looking at *Evening Sun* (p 89), *Aliki* (p 87), *F1* (p 94) and of course *Gas Station* (p 105).

In *Spata* (p 107) and *Underpass* (p 106), all trace of "incidents" seems to have disappeared to the benefit of the pure power of place—the kind of place that we sometimes come across, closed in on the enigma of its heavily meaningful presence. Such spaces are, as Walter Benjamin noted, real "scenes of crimes." What Benjamin wrote about Atget is strangely echoed, a century later, in Kokkinias' work: "It has justly been said that he photographed them [Paris streets] likes scenes of crimes. A crime scene, too, is deserted; it is photographed for the purpose of establishing evidence. With Atget, photographic records begin to be evidence in the historical trial [Prozess]. This constitutes their hidden political significance. They demand a specific kind of reception. Free-floating contemplation is no longer appropriate to them. They unsettle the viewer: he feels challenged to find a particular way to approach them."[2]

But what is this "specific kind of reception" today, and what might its "hidden political significance" be for today's viewers? As we saw, Michael Fried took the question of theatricality (or anti-theatricality) as one such access path, a touchstone of contemporary photography, by making Jeff Wall central to his ideas. And indeed, some of Panos Kokkinias' photographs are reminiscent of Wall's, notably *Cockroach* (p 111) and *Urania* (p 115) (the former evokes *Diagonal Composition*, [1993], and *Clipped Branches, East Cordova Street, Vancouver,* [1999], the latter, *Morning Cleaning, Mies van der Rohe Foundation, Barcelona,* [1999]). The idea here is obviously not to compare an artist to one of his famous predecessors, but to use what we may have understood about the former to cast light on new work. If we stick to the central question, as tirelessly formulated by Fried, it seems that Kokkinias' photographs are distinguished by a form of enigmatic exteriority and unreality which determines a form of anti-theatricality for the viewer. But even the works of his that seem closest to simple still lifes or innocuous, everyday scenes still have what could be called an added brilliance. Over the apparent banality is superimposed an undefined intention, a way of heightening the image without affirming a meaning, which distances us from a representation of everyday life and takes us into the register of dream and fantasy.

This might seem to contradict the title of an ensemble such as *Here We Are* (pp 73–115), for example. But if we look more closely, we realize that this title can be understood not as a statement of the obvious, but us a way of locating us in a state of imminence, in the expectation of what is coming. It is not the thingness of the thing that is in play, nor its capacity to elicit projections on the part of the viewer, in the manner of a minimalist "specific object." The reaction provoked here seems to be more one of uncertainty; as if something was not reaching completion, but could not be absorbed into one single notion. Everything is suspended, plunged in the artificial light that creates the effect of brightness evoked above. In *Leonidas* (p 93) the figure is literally enclosed in

a double circle; in *Dana* (p 28) the woman is caught between two zones of hazy color, from which she is emerging in the transparency of a rectangle, etc. As Katerina Gregos has appositely observed, "All of these paradoxical circumstances result in an ambiguous narrative that takes place somewhere in the space between fantasy, reality, paradox, and a dream-like state, which draws the viewer into a reflexive space, a mental space of projection, but perpetually denies him or her the possibility of a conclusion."[3] Personally, and although I find this suspension of meaning, this narrative deceptiveness, of the greatest interest, I would be tempted to place the emphasis more on the sensations produced by these images, the ones that arise not so much from the strangeness of the situations as from the artist's plastic choices. I spoke about color, but I should also mention, in the book, the juxtaposition of details with the complete reproductions of images. The detail is of course used to offset the modest size of the page format compared to that of the image being reproduced, and the consequent risk that the detail would go unnoticed in reproduction. But this also tells us something about the tension that pervades these photographs, between the scene of representation and the scene of sensation. What the eye perceives in the photograph is a field of colours and forms that constitutes a very powerful scenic device in its own right. The kind of zoom effect created by the reproduction of the detail in the book is an equivalent of the invitation extended to the beholder of the picture to enter into the image and identify the point where the narrative is clinched, the scene within the scene where the threads of the narrative or drama are woven together or untied.

But it is not certain that this is what happens, in a simple logic of focusing the gaze on a key detail, as is sometimes the case in Old Master paintings. The focus of the viewer's attention remains unpredictable, and it is on the basis of this relative indeterminacy that Kokkinias' work proposes a new relation between figure and ground, ensemble and detail. Here, of course, we need to bear in mind Daniel Arasse's remarkable study of the detail.[4] In the second half of his book especially, Arasse draws attention to the contradictions and oscillations induced by the effect of details: these make us oscillate between a distant and proximate view, undermining

the "distance point" that is meant to fix the ideal position for the beholder, in order to "elaborate an appearance of three-dimensionality conceived in relation with a fictive beholder."[5] The coming and going between distant and proximate vision that we perform in order to examine a detail destroys this fiction. The beholder becomes, as the art historian puts it, "dislocated," and from this "dialectic of dislocation" there emerges a veritable "temporal scansion," "an inscription of creative temporality within the painting, the inscription of an event of painting in the time of the gaze."[6]

It is thus this specific temporality of the gaze that is brought into play by the reproduction of details in the printed version of the work. No doubt this should be seen as an invitation to transpose this "dislocated" vision to our reading of the work itself, and perhaps even to consider that the work exists in two different modes—photographic print and printed book—each of which fuels our desire and expectation of the other. By a further irony, this paradox of detail operates within a practice, photography, which was precisely the medium that facilitated the perception of details in paintings, and made it possible to constitute them as objects of study. It is thus legitimate that the question of the relations between painting and photography should be reactivated here, as it has been constantly for over 170 years, around the "narrative temporalization" of two spaces of representation that sometimes coincide, and sometimes don't.

1. Michael Fried, *Why Photography Matters as Art as Never Before*, Yale University Press, 2008, p. 345.
2. Walter Benjamin, "The Work of Art in the Age of Mechanical Reproduction," 1939, in *Selected Writings III*, Cambridge: Belknap Press, p. 258.
3. Katerina Gregos, *"Unpredictable Incidents in Familiar Surroundings,"* exh. cat. Panos Kokkinias, Galerie Xippas, 2004.
4. Daniel Arasse, *Le Détail: Pour une histoire rapprochée de la peinture,* Paris: Flammarion/Champs, 1996.
5. Daniel Arasse, op. cit., p. 238.
6. Daniel Arasse, op. cit, p. 244.

Our Shared Circumstance

Susan Kismaric

The photographs gathered here have been organized by the photographer into four sections that he has entitled *Home, Interiors, Landscapes,* and *Here We Are,* the last of which brings a clear suggestion of confrontation with our existential state, the overarching theme of the book. The sections are porous because the sustained themes of the pictures, which are particularly contemporary ones, are those of anxiety and isolation, not to mention downright dread. The photographs are not fragments of ordinary, unmanipulated reality, snatched from the flow of everyday life, but, rather, they are oftentimes extraordinary, fantastical constructions completely arranged and orchestrated by Kokkinias. Handsomely composed, simple and pictorial, Kokkinias' photographs have been preconceived and are illustrations of the photographer's ideas.

The historical precedents for arranging and constructing photographs began in the nineteenth century and are particularly noteworthy during photography's so-called "Pictorialist" era mid-century when photographers made pictures whose subject matter was "important." Two notable early examples are the work of Oscar G. Rejlander (1813–1875) and Henry Peach Robinson (1830–1901). A Swedish photographer working in England, Rejlander was noted for his allegorical compositions made with the technique of "combination printing" in which he joined multiple negatives to form a single image. The most famous of these, *The Two Ways of Life* (1857) shows two young men on either side of an elder sage; one young man is turning towards representations of religion, charity, and industry while the other towards gambling and licentiousness, which end in suicide and death. The final print of the picture measures 16 x 31 inches and was compiled from individual photographs Rejlander made of groups of costumed people he hired and photographed at scales appropriate to the distance at which they would appear to the spectator of such a scene. Henry Peach Robinson (1830–1901), was a British portrait photographer who having begun as a painter also used "combination printing." Robinson's first and most famous composite picture is *Fading Away* (1858) in which a pale, dying young woman on a divan is tended by two other women, pre-

sumably family members, as a man stands at the window with his back to her and us, his anguished face, the picture suggests, too distressed for us to bear. In order to compete with the great themes of painting and genre photography as fine art, F. Holland Day (1864–1933) assumed the role of Jesus Christ in a series of self-portraits entitled *The Seven Last Words of Christ* (1898), in which he recruited his neighbors in Norwood, Massachusetts to stage an outdoor reenactment of the crucifixion.

This "directorial mode," as constructed photographs of this nature have been more widely known, is evident in the work of Duane Michals (b. 1932). The 1960s documentary aesthetic with which the individual views in Michals' works have been made accrue in true narrative fashion, as building blocks that create a story with a beginning, middle, and end. Michals' sequenced pictures describe an unfolding event as in *Chance Meeting* (1970) in which the impossibility of Michals having been witness to this ordinary event and photographed it as it unfolded is immediately apparent to the viewer. But this disbelief is suspended as one is drawn into the "episode," seduced by the factuality of the individual images, which is, in turn, counterbalanced by the fictive nature of the entire series. Contemporary examples of manipulated and arranged photographs include a great variety of works, from the staged stills of Cindy Sherman (b. 1954) in which she reinvented herself in a series of self-portraits to take on questions of female identity in the late twentieth century, to the elaborately staged tableaux of Gregory Crewdson (b. 1962) whose overtly cinematic pictures reek with theatrical lighting and saturated colors within the sweep of the cinematic overview.

Closer in sensibility to the work of Kokkinias, and perhaps closer in chronology, are the enigmatic views of Philip-Lorca diCorcia (b. 1951) whose pictures of largely cosmopolitan contemporary life are "arranged" or otherwise controlled by the photographer in less visible ways than the aforementioned. The pictures in diCorcia's monograph *A Story Book Life* (Twin Palms, 2003) are of mostly young people in domestic settings, or at leisure in the countryside. Their implied narratives hold a sense

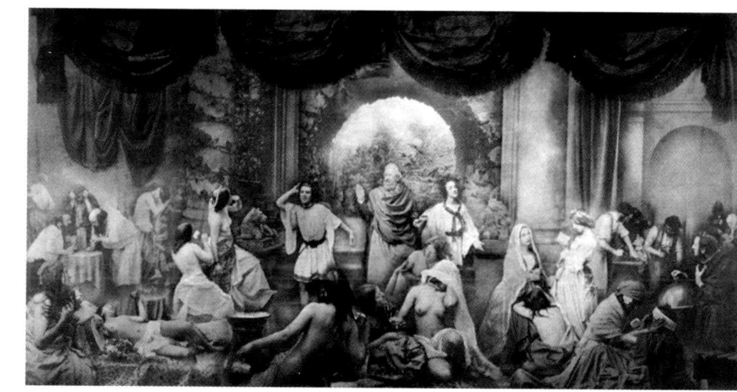

Oscar J. Rejlander, *The Two Ways of Life,* 1857

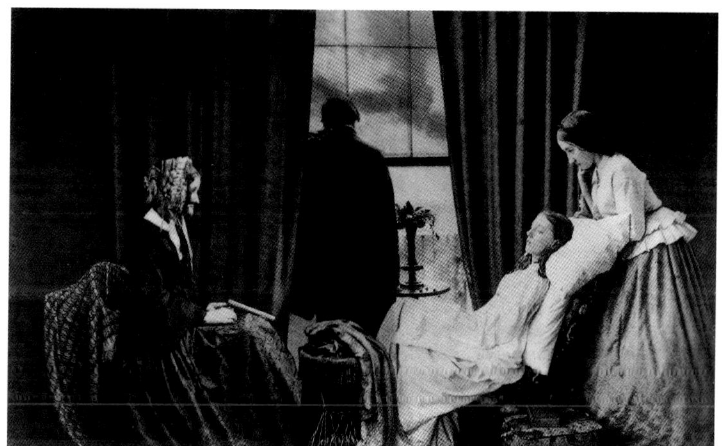

Henry Peach Robinson, *Fading Away,* 1858

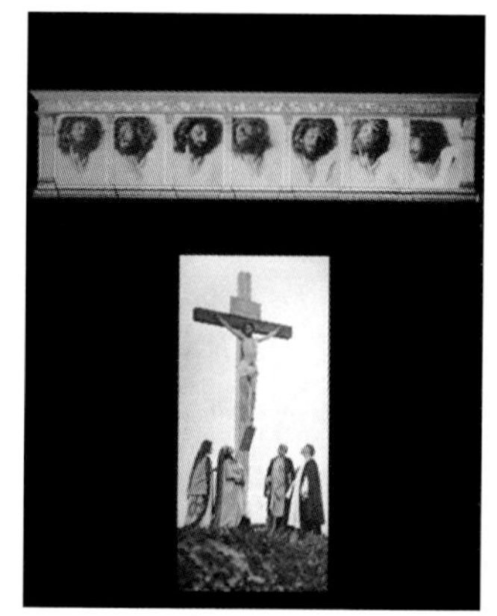

F. Holland Day, *The Seven Last Words of Christ,* 1898

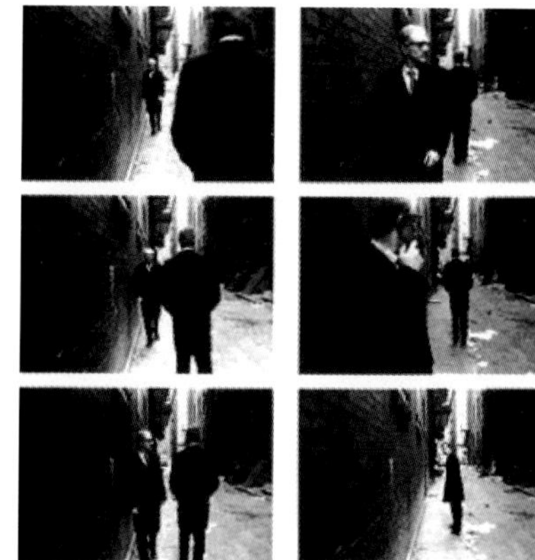

Duane Michals, *Chance Meeting,* 1970

of menace and certainly reveal a restless, discontented author whose anxieties are assuaged by little and who is redeemed from his existential despair only occasionally. Many of these pictures have been taken with a camera on a tripod which means that the action was not quite as spontaneous as they first might suggest and that diCorcia's subjects may have been "directed." In his floating *Noemi* (1989) a young woman lies on a raft amidst marshes, much like *Hamlet*'s Ophelia as seen in John Everett Millais' painting of 1851–1852, and as such the photograph is imbued with a portent of disaster.

The work of Kokkinias is a contemporary extension of this venerable tradition. A closer investigation of the particulars of his work reveals its allegiances to and departures from these precedents. Kokkinias avoids the painstaking labor of his nineteenth century counterparts Rejlander and Robinson by using the computer to create modern versions of "combination printing." Through simple pictures whose readings are immediate, Kokkinias conjures up the drawings in comic books or, perhaps, the storyboards made in preparation for the filming of a movie: the individual photographs represent individual scenes, declaratively stating their themes. The screeching neon colors of many of the pictures exacerbate our sense of alienation and, at the same time, emulate the exaggeration of comic drawing whereby images are purposefully reduced to their essence in terms of action and meaning to achieve more powerful impact. For example, in the photograph *Penelope* (p 99), a picture of a relatively young woman standing amidst commuters, the "drawing" of her figure is such that her countenance and facial expression refuses to tell us everything. She appears as though she has been struck by a terrible realization and has, literally, stopped in her tracks. The out-of-focus figures of the men in the foreground who frame her and the bright light on her, created by the artist through the use of a reflector, direct our attention to her. While the drawings in the individual panels of comic strips are intended to carry the plot forward, in Kokkinias' book, there is pointedly no forward momentum, just a deliberate recircling of themes.

In the book's first section, *Home*, which consists of photographs of domestic interiors—a site we like to think provides privacy and refuge—our commonly endured existential fears are fed. Middle-class life is evident in the furnishings, books, the corked half-bottle of wine, parquet floors, and the art postcards and calendar. The section begins with a dispiriting view of the interior of a refrigerator freezer. Who hasn't looked into their freezer with the false hope of finding something to cook only to find empty ice-cube trays and an abandoned hunk of frozen meat that will take twelve hours to defrost?

The man who appears in these pictures is an anonymous protagonist in the middle-class struggle to create a meaningful identity. The eerie calm in the series is abruptly disrupted when mayhem breaks through in *Cabinet* (p 13), the photograph in which we see the feet and lower legs of the man as he inexplicably stands on a dresser arranged with sea shells and corals gathered from distant shores sitting next to a stack of newspapers. The symbolic meaning of the picture is paramount. Has the man been reduced to simply another object in the benign, reassuring arrangement? In another photograph, the bare walls and clean lines of the room in which the man laughs uproariously, or madly, contributes to our sense that the room is, perhaps, institutional, so that our mirthful protagonist, dressed as he is in the uniform of institutional "whites" is simply mad. Since it is the last picture in the series, our sense of entrapment is complete and we leave the site of *Home* with the conviction that there is no solace there.

We then move into the next section of the book, *Interiors*, a series of pictures of the kinds of anonymous public spaces we encounter during the course of our daily lives. *Interiors* is a set of pictures made in public places, sites created by people for other people, in which the protagonists appear utterly alone or, in one picture, engaged in an awkward attempt at "connecting." Cold, lifeless hallways, a massive swimming pool and arena, and a mostly empty parking lot, among other sites, continue our sense of alienation. Foreboding is evident in the parking lot picture (p 37) because in moments a moving car is going to turn the corner and encounter a man on his hands and knees. The viewer is obliged to finish the narrative as he or she imagines it, which raises the voyeuristic aspect of the work, created at least partially by our photographic distance from the subjects (and it is here that the work bears a conceptual resemblance to that of Crewdson). One of the major aspects of photography, of course, is its inevitable "voyeuristic" nature, a quality that Kokkinias exploits to exaggerate his urgent "stories." We cannot help but feel that we have come upon a scene we should not, or would not, want to encounter. These include the toweled woman standing at the side of a pool as a man watches her without her knowing, or our view down an endless stairway where on a lower floor a couple engage in stand-up, clothed sex. The photographer and we, as unsuspecting viewers, are either voyeurs or innocent witnesses. In either case, we are implicated and the impulse is to act or flee.

By the time we enter the outdoors, pictures which comprise the third section of the book, *Landscapes*, we have moved from views of disturbing home sites and alienating public interiors to a both resplendent and forbidding "natural" world. The first picture describes blossomed trees within a verdant landscape. Amidst the foliage, we see a red-haired "Eve" as she contemplates the apple she has just bitten. But our Eve wears sunglasses, placing her several millennia after the original Eve, into our world. With the protagonists we travel across a variety of mostly uninhabited landscapes in which miniscule figures engage in an array of actions both bizarre and ordinary, raising questions about their intentions. Why is the man in the baseball cap so purposefully striding across a barren landscape in *Megalopolis* (p 48)? Craziness is seen in *Kastri* (p 55) in which someone photographs another man standing on a table in a large, evaporating pool of water in the countryside. The absurdity and mystery of their effort can, perhaps, be an illustration of the artist and his life, whilst the picture seems to suggest that art itself is folly. Finally, in *Mitsero* (p 67), did someone leap from their car into the polluted waters of a quarry? *Landscapes* ends with a photograph of a man trekking through a scorched forest dragging a chair as he continues his/our journey.

The straightforward title of the book's final section, *Here We*

Are, poses implicitly the question, "Where, exactly, is that?" Kok-kinias seems to suggest that we are in unidentified, deserted, industrialized landscapes, at home in bed, or driving behind a large truck with a butterfly trapped—not unlike us—in our windshield wiper, where, once again, we are the protagonist of the picture. We are the soccer goalie, standing before the goal and suffering anxiety before the kick, and we are a visitor with a nametag in the gleaming lobby of a corporate tower. And we are always alone. An air of mystery and menace permeates these pictures, precipitating our unease and dread. And again, within the refuge of home, we see a grandmother holding a sleeping child, both seemingly engaged in a kind of somnambulist activity, not quite part of this world.

As in the best works of art with difficult or distressing content, the sense of order imposed on the subject by the artist brings not only pleasure—as a sense of wonder at unleashed imagination and an appreciation of the scrupulous powers of execution—but also a simple, although brief, reprieve. Our contemporary anxieties and sense of alienation are momentarily at some distance having been identified for us by the artist and thrown into relief. Through Kokkinias' work, we are able to consider these small, human dramas that describe our commonly held fears and experiences with some objectivity and even, occasionally, to smile in response to our absurd position. Kokkinias confirms that our ills are inevitable and relentless, yet through his recognition, embrace and acceptance of them, we momentarily transcend their inevitability and our shared circumstance.

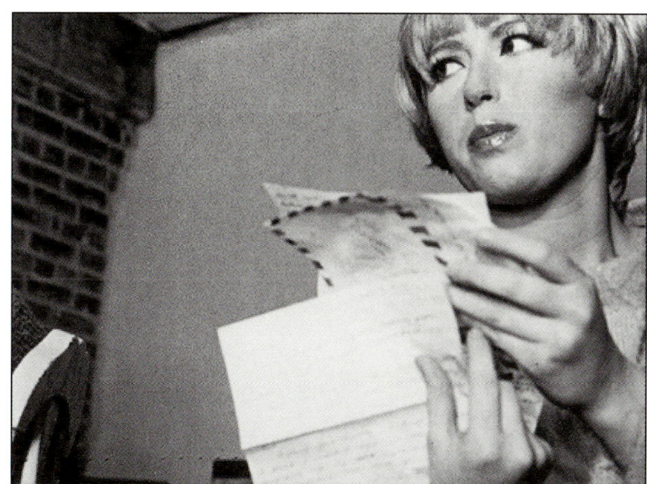
Cindy Sherman, *Untitled Film Still #5,* 1977

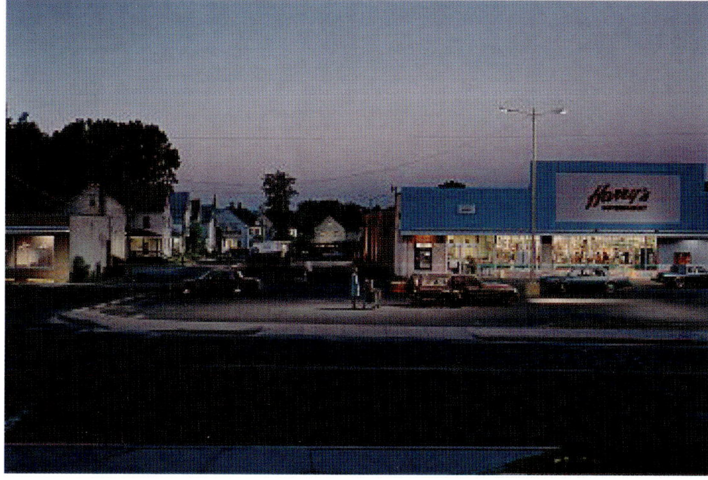
Gregory Crewdson, *Untitled,* 2004

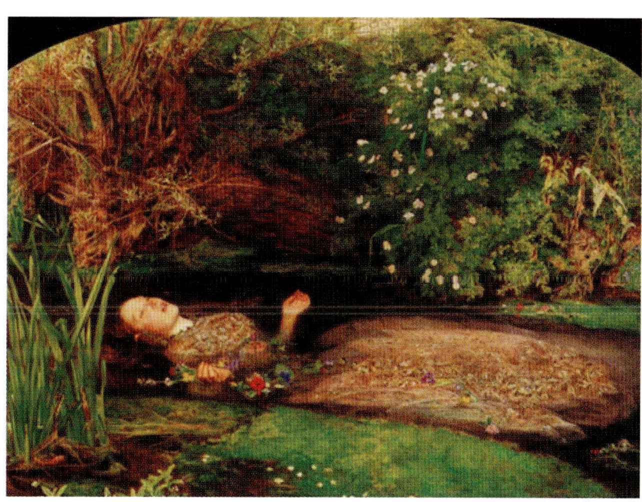
John Everett Millais, *Ophelia,* 1851–1852

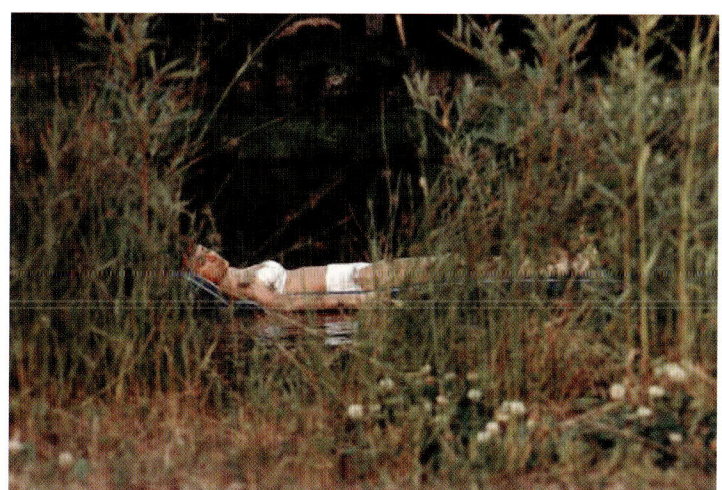
Philip-Lorca diCorcia, *Noemi,* 1989

Panos Kokkinias in Conversation with Alexandra Moschovi

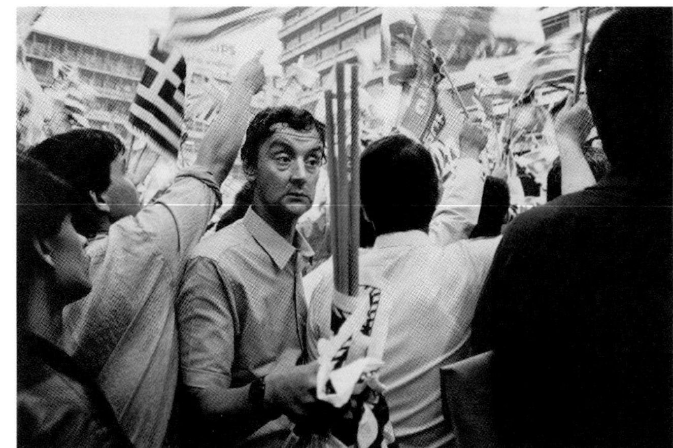

Athens, 1987

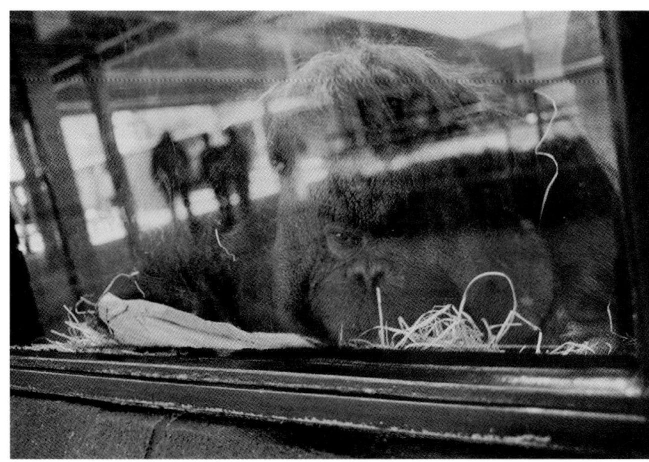

London, 1989

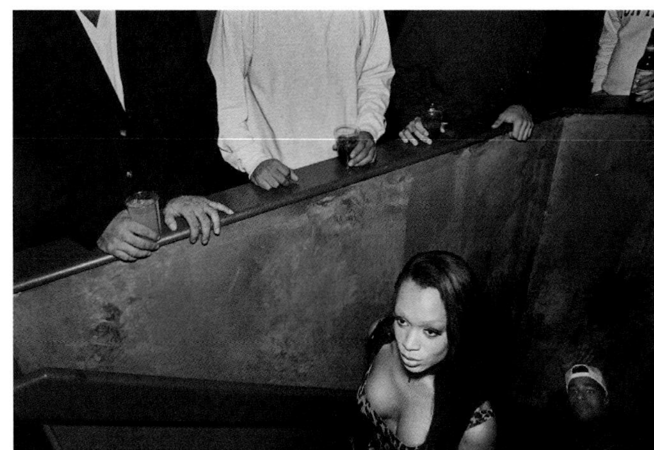

New York, 1993

Alexandra Moschovi: To begin with, let's talk about your formative years. What was it that led you to take up photography in the first place?

Panos Kokkinias: I was originally interested in cinema and thought that photography studies could be a way of sneaking into filmmaking through a, let's say, back door. But, getting more familiar with photography, I realized that it was a medium through which I could directly express myself without the need of a crew, intermediaries, or having to secure big funds. So I stayed with photography. Yet, I think that my initial interest in cinema survived and appeared later in my staged photographs.

A.M. There are indeed ontological affinities between the two media, but, apart from the obvious technical particularities, photography involves a distinctly different methodological approach and an equally disparate type of narrative to cinematography. How did the still, photographic image work for you as representation and means of self-expression so that it would eventually become for you an end in its own right?

P.K. Of course photography is quite different from cinematography, as it has to encapsulate the whole story in a single frame. And I think that this is what I was trying to do subconsciously, even in my early black-and-white work, perhaps as an exercise or preparation for a future cinematographic practice: to compress time in an autonomous micro-drama and create an instant with narrative qualities. I realize now that even when I was doing "straight" work my intention was not to capture or represent a slice of real time and space, but to project my own concerns onto reality.

A.M. This compression of time that maximizes drama, the fleetingness and serendipity of the flux of everyday life, the chance element, and "the simultaneous recognition, in a fraction of a second, of the significance of an event," as Henri Cartier-Bresson would put it in the 1950s, have long been the cornerstones of classic "straight," or "snapshot," practice, which also appear in your street work in the late 1980s. How did you position your

practice in relation to those traditions?

P.K. I started taking photographs in 1986 and until 1993 I followed different strands of this photographic tradition, solely in black and white. What I mostly admired was [Josef] Koudelka's existential persistence and Garry Winogrand's bravery to confront chaos through his paradoxical combination of humor and dread. My black-and-white photographs did not focus on specific subject matter but when I put them together to make a book, I realized that they were linked by a feeling of being lost in the world and creating a sense of fear. This was the sole distillation—if any—of my influences.

A.M. So, what was the drive behind the fairly momentous shift from straight, instantaneous photography towards the so-called "directorial," or otherwise constructed practice? How did you come to engineer the instantaneity of the seemingly "unmediated" document, what Jeff Wall came to term "near documentary?" Was it simply a change of heart?

P.K. Several different reasons and needs contributed to this change. The street theater that I had wished to encounter when I moved in New York City in the 1990s had already started to disappear as life was withdrawing from the streets and was moving indoors. At the same time people were becoming more and more aware of the camera being pointed at them, more suspicious about the intention of the operator and therefore more alert. And I started to have mixed feelings about using passersby without their consent. I gradually became tired of going after, or rather hunting, the "meaningful" out there. I did not have any more patience for things to happen. I started thinking that I could make them happen, but, then again, I would not dare to do such a thing until I went to Yale in 1994.

A.M. The 1990s was the time when the social aspect of photography and the boundaries between the private and the public were ardently reevaluated as photographers consciously retreated to the "pleasures and terrors of domestic comfort," as Peter Galassi would have it in the homonymous MoMA exhibition in the beginning of that decade. Part of your early directorial work was also enacted in the setting of the home with you as protagonist. How did this turn towards a more perfomative gesture for the camera come about?

P.K. I had seen Galassi's show and I was quite impressed by some of the works that I encountered there for the first time. I was really struck by [Philip-Lorca] diCorcia's *Mario* (1978), a picture of a man peering into his refrigerator, because it described an everyday moment that was very familiar to me. But such influences usually take time to fully develop, at least in my case. The shift came about progressively and out of my own needs. Tired of the streets, I began to photograph in New York nightclubs and gradually found myself making portraits of the peculiar characters that frequented those places. This led me to experiment, for the first time, with portraiture, a shift that coincided with the beginning of my graduate studies at Yale. This work was fairly problematic, as I could not come to terms with portraiture— I still haven't—and eventually the crisis I was experiencing with my photographic identity became a personal one. My reaction was to turn the camera towards myself as a way to reflect upon and resolve both personal and photographic issues. Homebound, due to an eating disorder, I could only photograph myself in the place where I was living at the time. And a self-portrait, as any portrait, is a staged picture. Anyway, this worked better, especially when I gradually started replacing my physical presence with surrogates for my psychological state. That's how *Home* came about, a series which, I believe, is more about a view of the world as prison rather than self-portraiture.

A.M. How did the creative environment at Yale, already established in the photographic world as the directorial mode school par excellence, affect this change? What were your influences?

P.K. To be honest, I was not really aware of what I was going into. Thomas Roma, my impassioned teacher at the School of Visual Arts in New York had suggested I go to Yale if I wanted to pursue graduate photographic studies after my first degree. I

was not aware at the time of the new staging "tradition" that was already being established there. I knew that Tod Papageorge was running the program and, knowing his work and of his close relationship with Garry Winogrand, I thought that I could continue and progress with what I was already doing. But, as I said, my need to change my modus operandi was very strong. The presence of Gregory Crewdson on the staff team at the school, the strong legacy that Philip-Lorca diCorcia had left behind, and the staged work of some of my classmates, created in a synergy that was instrumental in this change.

A.M. Going back to the conceptual attributes of the staged work, isn't the same personal psychological state of *Home* projected onto your models in *Interiors,* which is perhaps, correct me if I'm wrong, the first series in your body of work that attempts to encapsulate both the private and the public on the canvas of everyday life?

P.K. Although through *Home* I managed to escape into another kind of practice, and thereby overcome my photographic and personal impasse, the very circumstances that were behind the making of *Home* left a mark on me and this was inevitably reflected in the next series, *Interiors*. Despite the fact that I had eventually come out of the confines of my house, the sense of claustrophobia and imprisonment was still present in my succeeding attempts. What changed in *Interiors* was that while I was still making *Home* I started to look outside of the house. This began literally with *Crawling*, a picture I made from the window of my flat on the 17th floor. While homebound, I would spend hours looking out of this window, which was a way of connecting with the world outside. That's how I became interested in the distant human figure. This first picture depicted a man crawling on snow-covered pavement at night. Initially made as a metaphor for my situation, *Crawling* worked equally for me as an indicator for a way out and as a new photographic direction. It became the link between what I was doing at that moment and what I wanted to do next. What followed picked up on this double edge of private dramas in public spaces. The substitution of my house

for other interiors and of myself for these distant, often miniscule, figures allowed the transfer from the domestic entrapment to the anxious wandering within unfamiliar, yet equally seclusive and unescapable, surroundings.

A.M. The *Landscapes* series is an equally interesting photographic hybrid: it combines the conventions of lush, epic landscape photography with directorial practice, whilst, time and again, the same feeling of alienation from nature and self seems to run through as a unifying conceptual thread. How did you decide to take estranged city-dwellers out in the countryside?

P.K. When I returned to Athens, Greece, after six years of an "interior" life in the U.S., I felt the need to be out in the open taking advantage of the countryside and climate of Greece, which I had missed. I needed to reconnect with what constituted for me the essence of my country. Actually, my repatriation meant a whole different life, without the feeling of exile and weather that obliged me to stay indoors most days. I had to find a photographic excuse to be out there and my interest in the distant human figure was a perfect one. However, I did not want to make just colourful pictures of beautiful places. My long standing distaste for big cities was what fed and dictated my scenarios, which started to discuss the discomfort of modern man within the natural environment. I wanted to examine our deviation from nature and the consequent transfer of our urban neurosis to it whenever we find ourselves there.

A.M. What strikes me as a common characteristic in all three series we have discussed, which is also evident in your earlier street work, is a sense of ambiguity, both morphological and conceptual, which seems to reflect the endemic ambiguity of photography as representation.

P.K. Although photographs have only a remote relationship with reality, they do look like it and, therefore, like reality, they may have more than one interpretation. But an image open to different interpretations is different from one that aspires to remain unclear. Even if you want to talk about the lack of meaning in

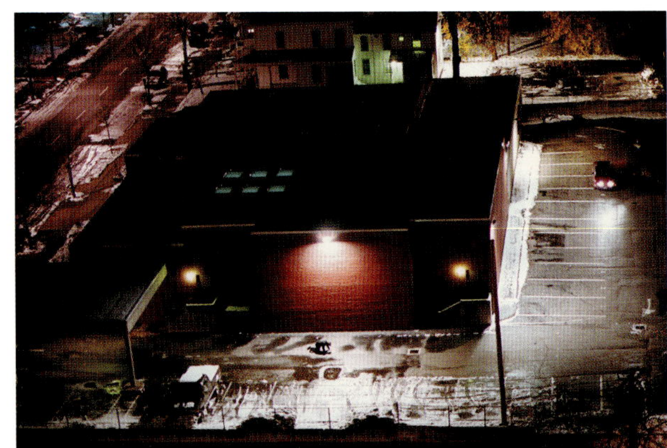

Crawling

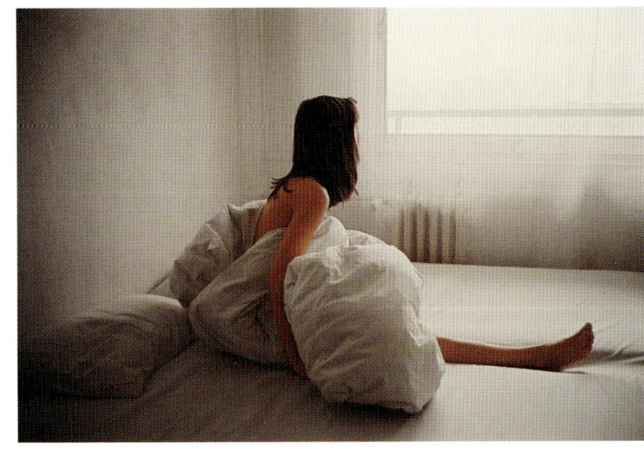

Kyriaki

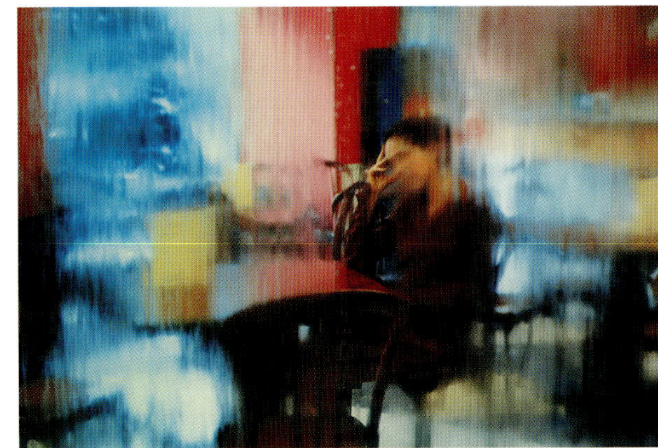

Diana

life, you have to use meaningful sentences. Poetry is not just some strange words put together. When I make a picture my intention is to articulate a concern of mine by photographic means as clearly as I can. More often than not this concern has to do with existential uneasiness and my scenarios evoke uncertainty, indecisiveness, nausea, and a sense of being lost in the world. This may be, and it has been, misunderstood as an intention to remain vague or unclear, so as to adhere to a pedestrian misconception about contemporary art: that art has to be, almost by definition, obscure, complicated, or difficult to understand. But I experience life as something very chaotic and this feeds my need to make sense of it. I have a strong, if not compulsive, tendency to put things in order just because I feel there is enough chaos around and inside me. And I think this tendency is, for better or worse, reflected in the morphological traits of my work. But ambiguity, as far as I am concerned, is not a means as such; it is a conclusion.

A.M. Is it right to say that this existential uneasiness is the overarching theme as denotation and connotation in your body of work?

P.K. I think that with the exception of *Landscapes*, where there is also a sociological and psychological touch, most of my work revolves around the old, perhaps outdated or banal for some, unanswered questions relating to the existential condition: the fact that we are here without knowing much about it. It is already there in the people lost in crowds and the imprisoned animals of the black-and-white work. It is there in the confinement of *Home*. It is there in *Interiors,* in the disorientated wandering of people in claustrophobic spaces. It is present as well in *Landscapes,* where the human figure is seen from afar and above, calling attention to our insignificance. And it is still present, this time more consciously, in the *Here We Are* series, in which the purposeful amalgamation of different genres aims to show that photography is a medium that can take on existential subject matter.

A.M. Yet, the existential condition that you describe is meant to

be, by definition, an esoteric condition, and thus invisible, some would even claim unrepresentable. How can one visualize the invisible in photographic terms?

P.K. By choosing subject matter that can accommodate existential interpretation and by choosing a method suitable to bring it out. For instance, the method used by Robert Frank in *The Americans*—consisting of his notational style, the imbalance of compositions, the open-ended and unfinished images—colors this book with an existential hue. The state of exile in many of Koudelka's pictures has a clear correlation with the human condition. Or, take Philip Lorca diCorcia's work, for example, in which a momentous realization inscribed on the face of an alienated pedestrian can be read as an existential epiphany. As far as I am concerned, I tried to make *Here We Are* by identifying notions relevant to the existential condition, such as wandering, nothingness, or death, and then finding situations that can visualize these notions in the widest possible variety of subjects. Therefore, I intentionally tried to mix as many different photographic genres as I could.

A.M. It is surprising how such disparate practices, from highly staged portraits (e.g., *Penelope,* p 99), meticulously orchestrated tableaux vivants (e.g., *Metro,* p 97) and hard-won still-lives (e.g., *Cockroach,* p 111) to diaristic snaps (e.g., *Kyriaki,* p 76), and overtly digital manipulated images (e.g., *Urania,* p 115), may produce such a seamless, multilayered narrative in *Here We Are*, one that wavers between reality and artifice, event and non event, chance and re-enactment, or even, to use Michael Fried's favorite distinction, "absorption" and "theatricality."

P.K. The seamlessness is facilitated by the common theme. When you put two pictures together, what matters more is what they are about, not how they were made. The osmosis that takes place blurs the distinction between the fabricated and the real, and even questions the necessity of making such a distinction. For instance *Kyriaki* (p 76), a diaristic note "taken" with a Leica camera and grainy film, when seen next to the staged *Diana* (p 91) acquires some of its sense of fiction. Likewise, *Diana* seen next to *Kyriaki* reads more as a picture that is taken quickly, if not snatched. One could further manipulate their reading by swapping their print sizes. Since size has become a co-signifier of artistic intention and milieu, it could well serve as a means to purposely mislead the viewer about the nature of a photograph. There are pictures in *Here We Are*, like *Hand* (p 80), *Butterfly* (p 79), or *Grave* (p 113), that are totally straight, that is, taken rather than made, and others like *Urania* (p 115) that could not have been conceived without counting on digital intervention. But the symbiosis of these different practices did not take place only at the level of putting them together in the same series. In several cases this fusion of methods took place within the pictures themselves. These hybrids combine, with varying proportions, straight, staged, and digital methods of image making. For example *Metro* (p 97) is a combination of reality and artifice as in an already existing crowd I physically integrated actors and then digitally manipulated the whole scene. *Penelope* (p 99) is a combination of street photography with portraiture. *Cockroach* (p 111) is a "snap" taken with a view camera and studio lights. I think that these varying degrees of staging and manipulation help the smooth transition between the different pictures, whilst the recurring overlap between these disparate photographic practices cross-fertilizes such seemingly "incompatible" genres.

A.M. *Here We Are* transgresses not only photographic genres but also iconographic/iconoclastic traditions, media, and disciplines, from surrealist imagery and post-war figurative painting to photo-conceptualism, from film noir and popular narrative cinema to contemporary performance, from existential literature and dramaturgy to ideas around supermodernity and the notion of the "non-place." Was this plurality and cross-referencing of pictorial and literary quotations equally a conscious decision?

P.K. The cultural baggage you carry is unavoidably transcribed in the work you do. Sometimes it is a conscious decision; sometimes things pop up in your head because they just do. Cross-fertilization is like making a soup. You don't have to follow a specific recipe; you can improvise and use whatever you have in the fridge, as long as you like cooking and you know how to cook.

A.M. You have been long challenging ideas around photography's unique phenomena and verisimilitude, whether these are physically rooted in its indexicality, or conceptually constructed around the modernist idea of taking rather than making photographs, but, in essence, you have retained this verisimilitude at the core of your practice, moving from one reality to another. What is it that you want to manifest?

P.K. Photography depends on the real, but it is not reality. This is why I am trying to retain a sense of verisimilitude while I do not feel obliged to achieve this solely through documentary work. I do not want to manifest anything and it is not my first priority to question the nature of the medium. Yet, the depiction of our contemporary condition requires contemporary methods that can register exactly what we experience now. This depiction is directly related to, and can be enhanced by, the use of what the medium can do today. Photography as we used to know it could visualize the human condition only as an imprint of the real through the act of taking a picture. But the real we experience today has changed. It is often mediated by the images we see every day on television, in the press, or on the Internet. The representation of the real has become part of the real. The indexical nature of photography, which used to constitute its very ontology, can no longer exclusively sustain such a representation. The imprint of the real is still there but whether it is obtained by taking or making a picture is not the issue any longer. And this is reflected by the multifaceted nature of contemporary photography and the increasing overlap between various photographic practices. The title *Here We Are* is thus a statement that carries an existential connotation not only on a philosophical but also on a photographic level. As an affirmation uttered to introduce the question that usually follows, that is, "What do we do now?," the title refers as well to the historical crossroads at which photography stands today.

A.M. So what's next?

P.K. There is almost always a picture in a previous series of work that leads me to what I do next. What I would like to pursue more persistently now is the direction of *Urania* (p 115). It is a pattern of work in which the intervention of digital manipulation, albeit evident, is not by any means the main theme, but facilitates the creation of fiction through the use of realistic tools. Although a fiction film may be more realistic than a photograph, we never judge it for not being "true." We judge it on the basis of how the reality it presents discusses real life. In this respect, I would like to see photography being absolved from its congenital and false identification with reality. Again, photography is not life; it is about life. No more and no less than that.

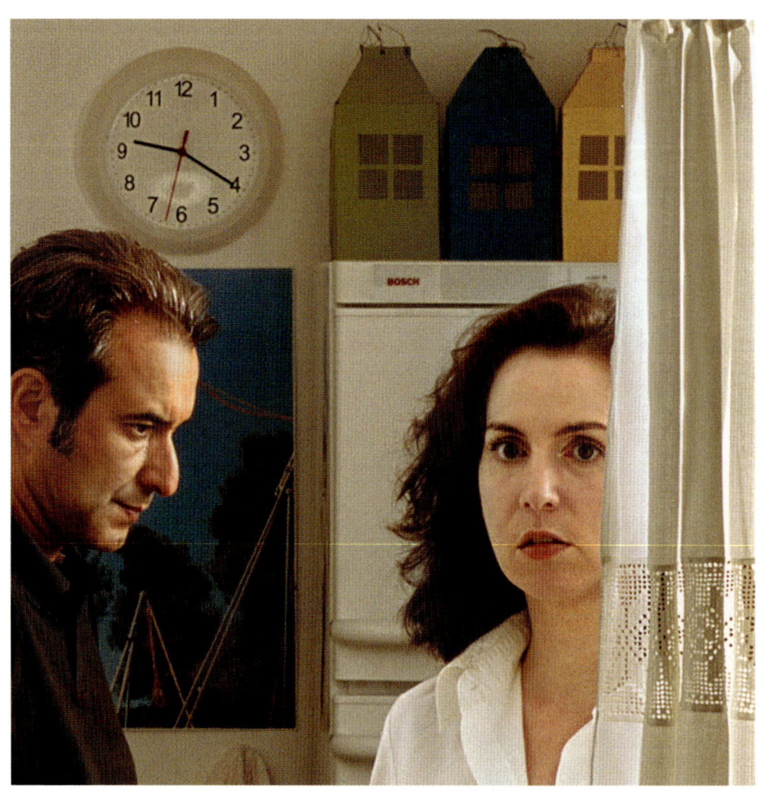

126 / Twenty Past Nine (detail)

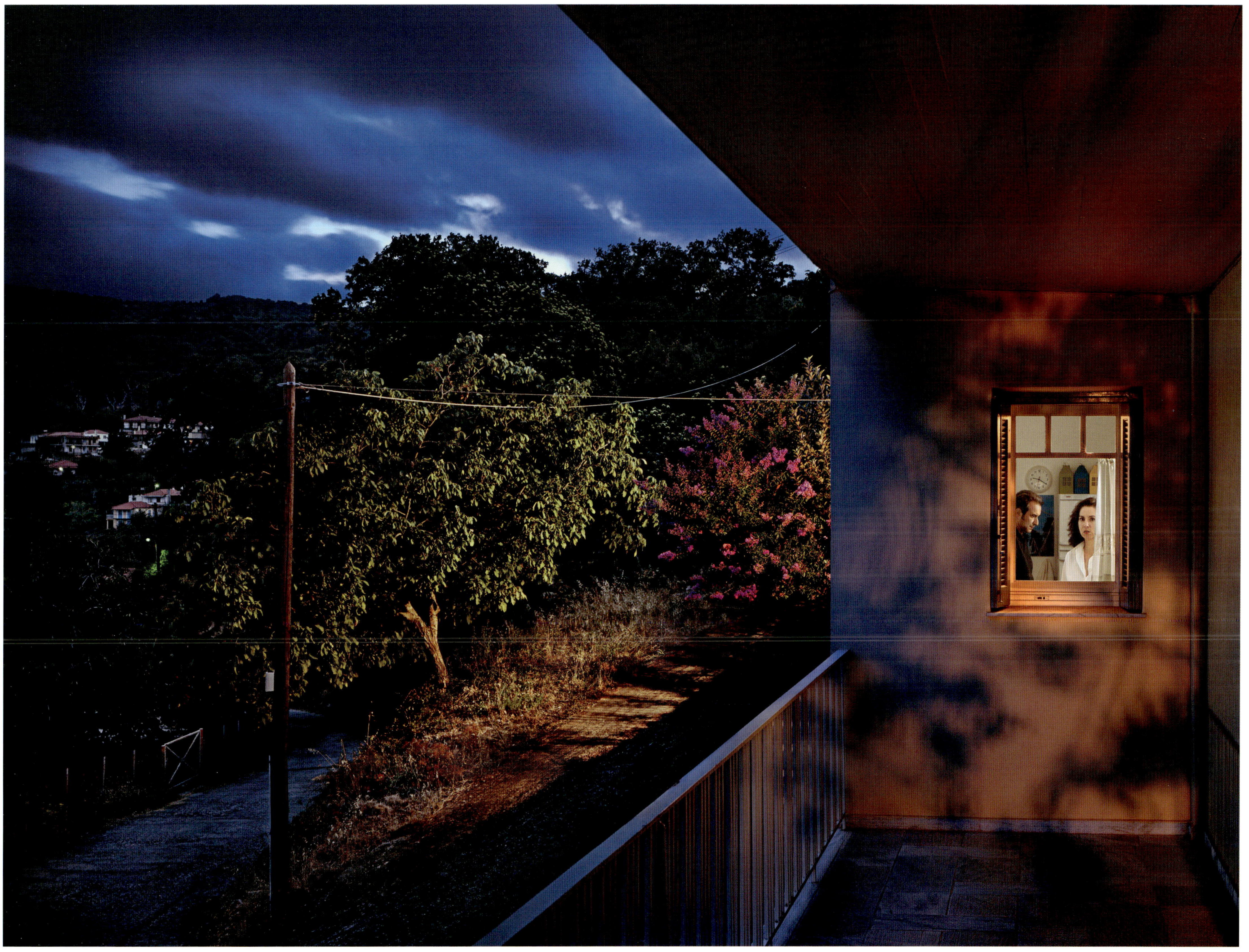

Biography

Born on July 4, 1965, in Athens, Greece.

Education

2009: School of Art, University of Derby, Derby, U.K., Ph.D.

1996: Yale School of Art, Yale University, New Haven, CT, U.S.A, M.F.A.

1993: School of Visual Arts, New York, NY, U.S.A, B.F.A.

Awards

2011: Book Publication Grant, Stavros Niarchos Foundation.

2000: Scholarship, State Scholarships Foundation, Greece.

1996: Ward Cheney Award, Yale University.

1995: Scholarship, Yale School of Art.

1995: Scholarship, Alexander Onassis Foundation.

Solo Exhibitions

2011: Galerie Xippas, Athens

2007: Galerie Xippas, Paris

2007: Galerie Xippas, Athens

2006: Findings, in Present Future d' Artissima 13, Lingotto Fiere, Turin, Italy

2005: Human Nature, Athens International Airport.

2004: Galerie Xippas, Paris.

2003: F1, 365 Art Project, Athens.

2001: Kappatos Gallery, Athens.

1998: Kappatos Gallery, Athens.

1993: Photohoros Gallery, Athens.

Selected Group Exhibitions

2011: The Eye Is A Lonely Hunter: Images Of Humankind. Fotofestival Mannheim, Ludwigshafen, Heidelberg. Germany.

2010: Time Within Us, Istanbul Museum of Modern Art, Turkey; Moscow House of Photography, Russia; Thessaloniki Museum of Photography, Greece.

2009: Realities and Plausibilities. Re-enacting Realism in Contemporary Photographic Art. Curated by Alexandra Moschovi, Xippas gallery, Athens, Greece.

Face to Faces. 2nd Thessaloniki Biennale of Contemporary Art, Thessaloniki Museum of Photography, Greece. 2009

Auto. Sueno y Materia. Automobile culture as critical and creative territory. Centro de Arte 2 de Mayo, Madrid, Spain.

2008: Aspects De La Photographie Hellenique, Saison Culturelle Européenne, Nice, France

And Now? Visual Arts in Greece 3, State Museum of Contemporary Art, Thessaloniki.

2007: In Present Tense, National Museum of Contemporary Art, Athens.

Recall Athens, a.antonopoulou.art gallery, Athens.

Dialogues Méditerranéens, Etés culturels de Saint-Tropez.

The Athens Effect, Maison Européenne de la Photographie, Paris.

Opening Hours, organized by Rebecca Camhi Gallery, Athens.

2006: Present Future, Artissima 13, Lingotto Fiere, Torino.

The Scarecrow, Averoff Museum of Modern Greek Art, Metsovo, Greece.

2004: Catch the light, Cultural events, Olympic Games ATHENS.

Ausderferne ausdernähe ausdermitte, European Patent Office, Munich.

Everyday Hellas, White Box Gallery, New York.

The Mediterraneans, MACRO, Rome.

Self-aboutness, Canal Isabel II, Hola Grecia! ARCO 2004, Madrid

Zeitgenössische Fotokunst (touring exhibition), Neuer Berliner Kunstverein, Berlin.

2003: Outlook, Cultural Olympiad, Benaki Museum, Athens 2000

(Un)familiar City, 7th International month of photography, Athens.

Photosynkyria, Macedonian Museum of Contemporary Art, Thessaloniki.

1999: The Conclusion of Paradox, Kapernekas Fine Arts, New York.

Communautés, Galerie Du chateau d' Eau, Toulouse, France.

Metro, DESTE Foundation, Athens.

1998: Photography Circle, Athens.
1997: New Narratives, Laurence Miller Gallery, New York.
Image and Icon, Macedonian Museum of Contemporary
Art, Thessaloniki.
1993: Mentors Show, Art Directors Club, New York.
1989: Eleven Greek Photographers, Montreal, Canada.
1988: Biennale for Young European Artists, Bologna, Italy.

Selected Bibliography

Moschovi, Alexandra. Realities and Plausibilities, Galerie Xippas, Athens, 2009.

Demos TJ. Vitamin Ph: New Perspectives in Photography. Phaidon Press, London, 2006.

Hoffmeister B, Tramboulis T. (eds.), The Athens Effect. Mudima Foundation, Milan, 2006.

Daniylopoulou Olga. The Scarecrow. Averoff-Tossizza Foundation, Metsovo, 2006.

Gregos, Katerina. Panos Kokkinias (monograph). Galerie Xippas. Paris, 2004.

Schoenert K., Bahtsetzis S., Moutsopoulos T., Ausderferne ausdernähe ausdermitte. European Patent Office, Munich, 2004.

Karra Marilena. Self-aboutness. Hola Grecia! ARCO 2004, Madrid.

Papaioannou Hercules. Zeitgenössische Fotokunst Aus Griechenland. NBK, Berlin, 2004.

Joachimides Christos (ed.). Outlook, Athens, 2003.

Moschovi, Alexandra. "(Un)familiar City". 7th International Month Of Photography. Athens, 2000.

Gregos, Katerina. "Art at Work". The Athenaeum Inter-continental Collection of Contemporary Greek Art, Athens, 2000.

Cameron, Dan. "The other side of now" Metro: New trends in contemporary Greek art. Deste Foundation, Athens, 1999.

Stathatos, John. Image and Icon. Macedonian Museum Of Contemporary Art, Thessaloniki, 1997.

Trachtenberg, Alan. Papageorge, Tod. Not from concentrate, Graduate Photography at Yale. New Haven, 1996

Rivellis, Platon. Panos Kokkinias, Sinking (monograph). Photohoros, Athens, 1993.

Selected Articles and Reviews

Kotzamani, Marina. 'Athens in the Twenty-First Century', PAJ: A Journal of Performance and Art - Volume 31, Number 2, May 2009, MIT Press, pp 20-22

Moschovi, A. "The Burden of Self-consciousness, exhibition review, a: The Athens Contemporary Art Review, no. 13, May-June, 2007, pp. 24-33

Kallitsis C. "Panos Kokkinias", Vlepo, no 2, Thessaloniki, (Oct. 2006),

Baqué, Dominique. "Melancolies", Art Press, (May 2004), p. 90.

Tselou, Katerina. "Interview with Panos Kokkinias", Artime no 1, Athens, (Oct. 2004), pp. 76 - 82.

Gregos, Katerina. "International News-Athens", Contemporary (Summer 2002), p. 34.

Koroxenidis, Alexandra. "Landscapes serve as world's stage", Kathimerini English Edition, Athens (Dec. 10, 2002).

Papadopoulou, Christy. "Man and Nature" Athens News, (Nov. 30 2002).

Aletti, Vince. "Voice Choices" The Village Voice, New York (Aug.12 1997).

Leger, Christophe. "Sinking" Iris no. 9, Paris (Summer 1994), p. 2.

Public And Corporate Collections

Société Générale, Paris, France.
Fundación Telefonica, Madrid, Spain.
Musée de la Roche-sur-Yon, France.
European Patent Office, Munich, Germany.
ADAC Collection, Munich, Germany.
Yale University Art Gallery, New Heaven, CT, USA.
Macedonian Museum of Contemporary Art, Thessaloniki, Greece.
Thessaloniki Museum of Photography, Greece.
Athenaeum Inter-Continental, Athens, Greece.

List of Works

All color work: Digital C-prints

02 Niagara: 80 x 120 cm / 31.5 x 47 in

Home 1994-95
07 Freezer: 70 x 90 cm / 27 x 35 in
08 Milk: 80 x 100 cm / 31.5 x 40 in
09 Meat: 80 x 109 cm / 31.5 x 43 in
10 Peanuts: 50 x 75 cm / 20 x 30 in
11 Spaghetti: 90 x 60 cm / 36 x 24 in
12 Shower Cap: 80 x 100 cm / 31.5 x 40 in
13 Cabinet: 60 x 90 cm / 24 x 36 in
14 T.V.: 50 x 75 cm / 20 x 30 in
15 Smoke: 50 x 75 cm / 20 x 30 in
17 Laughter: 14 x 21 cm / 5.5 x 8 in

Interiors 1995-96
21 Grand Central: 145 x 100 cm / 57 x 39 in
22 Blue Room: 80 x 110 cm / 31.5 x 43 in
23 Squash: 80 x 112 cm / 31.5 x 44 in
24 Push-pin: 80 x 112 cm / 31.5 x 44 in
25 Skylight: 80 x 110 cm / 31.5 x 43 in
26 Tom: 80 x 105 cm / 31.5 x 42 in
27 Hans: 80 x 110 cm / 31.5 x 43 in
28 Dana: 80 x 110 cm / 31.5 x 43 in
29 Brian: 80 x 105 cm / 31.5 x 42 in
31 Swimming Pool: 80 x 110 cm / 31.5 x 43 in
32 Dog: 50 x 75 cm / 20 x 30 in
33 Laura: 80 x 105 cm / 31.5 x 42 in
35 Twins: 120 x 157 cm / 47 x 62 in
37 Crawling: 60 x 90 cm / 24 x 36 in

Landscapes 1997-
41 Megla: 120 x 120 cm / 47 x 47 in
42 Pafos: 120 x 158 cm / 47 x 62 in
43 Chalandriani: 120 x 168 cm / 47 x 66 in
45 Argalastiz: 120 x 173 cm / 47 x 68 in

47 Circle: 120 x 157 cm / 47 x 62 in
48 Megalopolis: 120 x 163 cm / 47 x 64 in
49 Dragouni: 120 x 160 cm / 47 x 63 in
51 Lefkonas: 120 x 170 cm / 47 x 67 in
52 Aghida: 120 x 154 cm / 47 x 60 in
53 Vardia: 120 x 160 cm / 47 x 63 in
55 Kastri: 120 x 157 cm / 47 x 62 in
57 Menalo: 120 x 156 cm / 47 x 61 in
58 Lambinou: 120 x 157 cm / 47 x 62 in
59 Kokkinovrahos: 120 x 163 cm / 47 x 64 in
61 Kostas: 120 x 170 cm / 47 x 67 in
63 Kremasmata: 120 x 156 cm / 47 x 61 in
65 Fanos: 120 x 160 cm / 47 x 63 in
67 Mitsero: 120 x 136 cm / 47 x53 in
69 Ypato: 120 x 154 cm / 47 x 60 in
71 Syrna: 120 x 150 cm / 47 x 59 in

Here We Are 2002-07
75 Itea: 120 x 170 cm / 47 x 67 in
76 Kyriaki: 40 x 60 cm / 16 x 24 in
77 Hospital: 104 x 80 cm / 41 x 31.5 in
79 Butterfly: 27 x 40 cm / 11 x 16 in
80 Hand: 18 x 27 cm / 7 x 10.5 in
81 Deck: 18 x 27 cm / 7 x 10.5 in
83 Theoni: 158 x 120 cm / 62 x 47 in
85 Goalkeeper: 120 x 167 cm / 47 x 66 in
87 Aliki: 120 x 177 cm / 47 x 70 in
89 Evening Sun: 120 x 183 cm / 47 x 72 in
91 Diana: 120 x 160 cm / 47 x 63 in
93 Leonidas: 120 x 163 cm / 47 x 64 in
94 F1: 120 x 153 cm / 47 x 60 in
95 Naomi: 120 x 156 cm / 47 x 61 in
97 Metro: 100 x 303 cm / 39 x 119 in
99 Penelope: 120 x 155 cm / 47 x 61 in
101 Alexandros: 120 x 158 cm / 47 x 62 in
103 Rain: 153 x 120 cm / 60 x 47 in
105 Gas Station: 127 x 230 cm / 50 x 91 in

106 Underpass: 127 x 154 cm / 50 x 60 in
107 Spata: 127 x 174 cm / 50 x 68 in
109 Piraeus: 127 x 183 cm / 50 x 72 in
111 Cockroach: 120 x 170 cm / 47 x 67 in
112 Amorgos: 14 x 21 cm / 5.5 x 8 in
113 Grave: 27 x 40 cm / 11 x 16 in
115 Urania: 120 x 156 cm / 47 x 62 in

Interview with A. Moschovi (Gelatin Silver prints)
122 Athens 1987: 21 x 32 cm / 8.5 x 12.5 in
122 London 1989: 21 x 32 cm / 8.5 x 12.5 in
122 New York 1993: 21 x 32 cm / 8.5 x 12.5 in

127 Twenty Past Nine: 120 x 162 cm / 47.64 in

Acknowledgements

Thanks to: Stavros Niarchos Foundation, Yerassimos Yannopoulos, Thomas Roma, Tod Papageorge, Renos Xippas, Alexandra Moschovi, Vicky Lemoni, Michalis Varouxis. *-P.K.*

This publication was made possible with the support of Niarhos Foundation; www.SNF.org

ΙΣΝ SΝf STAVROS NIARCHOS FOUNDATION

All photographs courtesy of the artist and Xippas Gallery; www.xippas.com

xippas gallery

Cover picture: Semiramis Hotel, Athens.

Contributors' Biographies

Régis Durand has worked alternatively in the academic and art worlds. A University Professor, he has also written extensively on photography and contemporary art, and curated many exhibitions. He was artistic director of the Printemps de Cahors (1992–1996), Director of the Centre national de la photographie in Paris (1996–2003), and Director of the Jeu de Paume, Paris (2003–2006). Now an independent curator and consultant, he has recently been appointed Director of the Printemps de Septembre à Toulouse.

Susan Kismaric, Curator in the Department of Photography at The Museum of Modern Art, New York, joined the Museum in 1976. Kismaric has organized many exhibitions for the Museum, most recently, *Shimmer of Possibility: Photographs by Paul Graham,* which was on view in spring 2009. Other exhibitions organized by Kismaric include *Present Tense: Photographs by JoAnn Verburg* (2007), and *Photographs* by Larry Fink (1980), among many others. The author and editor of the books and catalogs accompanying these shows, she has also contributed essays to other publications issued by the Museum, most recently *Modern Women: Women Artists at The Museum of Modern Art* (2010). She has been a visiting Senior Critic of Photography at the Yale School of Art since the early 1980s and is currently teaching a history of post-World War II American photography class at Fordham University.

Alexandra Moschovi is a researcher, editor, curator, author, and lecturer on photographic theory at the University of Sunderland in the U.K. She earned a BA in Photography from the School of Fine Arts and Design, T.E.I. of Athens, Greece; an MA in Communications from Goldsmiths College, London; and a PhD in Art History from Courtauld Institute of Art, London. Her writing has appeared in multiple publications, and she co-edited a book released in 2007, *I Ellada mesa apo ti Fotografia: 160 Chronia Optikes Martyries* (Greece through Photographs), by Melissa Publishing, Athens.

Here We Are

Photographs © 2012 Panos Kokkinias
"The Determinate and Indeterminate Gaze in the Photographs of
Panos Kokkinias" Essay © 2012 Régis Durand
"Our Shared Circumstance" Essay © 2012 Susan Kismaric
Interview © Alexandra Moschovi

Published in the United States by powerHouse Books, a
division of powerHouse Cultural Entertainment, Inc.
37 Main Street, Brooklyn, NY 11201-1021
telephone: 212.604.9074, fax: 212.366.5247
email: hereweare@powerhousebooks.com
website: www.powerhousebooks.com

First edition, 2012

Library of Congress Control Number: 2011941979

Hardcover ISBN 978-1-57687-574-2

Printing and binding by RR Donnelley, China
Book design by Panos Kokkinias, with thanks to Michalis
Varouxis and powerHouse Books.

A complete catalog of powerHouse Books and Limited Editions is
available upon request; please call, write, or visit our website.

10 9 8 7 6 5 4 3 2 1

Printed and bound in China